Proclamation and Praise

Proclamation and Praise

*Hebrews 2:12 and
the Christology of Worship*

RON MAN

Wipf & Stock
PUBLISHERS
Eugene, Oregon

PROCLAMATION AND PRAISE
Hebrews 2:12 and the Christology of Worship

ISBN 13: 978-1-55635-056-6

Manufactured in the U.S.A.

Dedication

To the memory of the late Prof. James B. Torrance of Scotland, whose writings first introduced me to the wondrous concept of Christ leading our worship, this volume is affectionately and gratefully dedicated.

Contents

Introduction

THE SO-CALLED "worship wars" continue unabated in our midst. In all too many quarters, serious biblical discussions on worship have been abandoned in favor of a relentless pursuit of "what works."

What is needed above all in our day is a broadening examination of unifying theological concepts of worship—trans-cultural, trans-congregational, trans-denominational. We should be asking: What are biblical truths about worship which are non-negotiable—which we may only apply, not reject or change? What are those aspects of worship about which we can all potentially agree, even while we in grace allow for differing applications of those truths in different local bodies?

William Nicholls understands what is at stake when he writes: "To embark upon a study of the meaning, or essence, of worship is to embark upon a quest for the substance of Christian unity."[1] His approach is to seek "a point at which the central concerns of the different traditions with which we are acquainted can be creatively related to each other."[2] We may well wonder whether we are "creative" enough to span the chasms which divide us; but Nicholls suggests that we need to look to Christology. He writes:

> The foundation of Christian worship is our Lord Himself, as the One who is both the di-

1. Nicholls, *Jacob's Ladder*, 12.
2. Ibid.

vine Word and man's perfect response to that Word. If we make it our endeavour, as we think of the different aspects of worship, to recognize His work, we shall find the essence of worship, as well as the true concern of the different traditions, and also the unity which our divisions obscure.[3]

Lofty ambitions, to be sure, but surely this is the direction in which we should be heading: rather than staking out our sectarian claims to the "right" way to worship, we should be seeking out common biblical ground which is indeed non-negotiable but also universally applicable. Nicholls would lead us to the Person and work of Christ:

Our aim will be to relate worship at every point to the revelation and redemption which God brought about in Christ, and to show how He is the *Jacob's Ladder* upon which passes all that traffic of God to man and man to God which is the meaning of our worship.[4]

This paper will seek to follow Nicholls' lead and advice by examining a key passage relating to the Christology of worship. It is found in the Epistle of Hebrews, the New Testament book which has more to say about worship than any other (with the possible exception of Revelation). The passage to be unpacked is Hebrews 2:12, which in its immediate context reads:

[11]For both He who sanctifies and those who are sanctified are all from one Father; for which reason He is not ashamed to call them brethren, [12]saying, "I will proclaim Your name to my brethren, in the midst of the congregation

3. Ibid.
4. Ibid.

I will sing Your praise." [13]And again, "I will put my trust in Him." And again, "Behold, I and the children whom God has given me." (Heb 2:11–13 NASB)[5]

This passage, and especially the Old Testament quotation in verse 12, has tremendous and far-reaching implications for how we understand the Church, her Head and her worship. It will be argued that 2:12 serves as a key to unlocking the Christological dimensions of New Covenant worship. It is this writer's hope and prayer to encourage more awareness of the precious truth that *the Lord Jesus is living and active in our midst as the Mediator of God's truth and the Leader of our worship.*

---

5. Unless otherwise noted, Scripture references are from the ESV.

The Context
of Hebrews 2:12

The Context of the Book of Hebrews

CALVIN FITTINGLY captured some of the depth and majesty of the Epistle to the Hebrews when he wrote in
the introduction to his commentary:

> There is, indeed, no book in Holy Scripture which
> speaks so clearly of the priesthood of Christ,
> which so highly exalts the virtue and dignity of
> that only true sacrifice which He offered by His
> death, which so abundantly deals with the issue
> of ceremonies as well as their abrogation, and, in
> a word, so fully explains that Christ is the end of
> the Law. Let us therefore not allow the Church
> of God or ourselves to be deprived of so great a
> benefit, but firmly defend the possession of it.[1]

Striking for its uniquely expansive treatment of the
priestly ministry of Christ,[2] the epistle was a rallying
point for John Calvin in his zeal to restore an apostolic

1. Calvin, *Hebrews and the First and Second Epistles of St. Peter*, 1.
2. "It is mainly to St. Paul that we turn for our understanding of
the priesthood of the Church . . . and mainly to the Author of the
Epistle to the Hebrews that we turn for our understanding of the
High Priesthood of Christ" (T. F. Torrance, *Royal Priesthood*, 10).

Christology to the Christian Church.[3] Philip Edgcomb Hughes, as well as many others, holds that "the comprehensive theme of the Epistle to the Hebrews is that of the absolute supremacy of Christ."[4]

Evangelicals rightly focus on the atoning death of Christ as the price paid for our redemption and the reason for the hope that is within us. Yet an aspect of Christ's Person and ministry that is too often neglected is that of His *present* work. Hebrews especially testifies to this continuing ministry of Christ, as well as of course emphasizing the once-for-all completion and abrogation of the Old Covenant system by His completed work on the cross. The crucified, risen and glorified Savior has accomplished His saving work; but that does not mean that He has gone into a sort of "cosmic retirement." Hughes and Chafer concur:

> To picture Christ as seated in glory is not of course to suggest that he is now inactive. . . . The heavenly existence of the exalted Savior may be described as one of ceaseless activity. He is . . . constantly sustaining the universe. . . . He rules over history. . . . On behalf of his chosen people he dispenses mercy, grace, and help. . . . "He always lives to make intercession for them" ([Heb] 7:25).[5]

> His entrance into heaven was a great triumph, signifying the completion of His work on earth, and an entering into His new sphere of work at the right hand of the Father.[6]

3. Calvin, *Hebrews and the First and Second Epistles of St. Peter*; Calvin, *Institutes* 2.15.6.

4. Hughes, *Hebrews*, 2.

5. Ibid. Hughes neglects to include in his list, however, Christ's role in our worship.

6. Chafer, *Major Bible Themes*, 71.

Christopher Cocksworth maintains that Hebrews'
"Christological and doxological attention to the status of
Christ should not distract us from the overriding thrust of
the book which is about how Christ leads us into the holy
presence of God."[7]

The Immediate Context: Apostle and High Priest (3:1)

A number of commentators have pointed out how Hebrews
3:1 ("consider Jesus, the Apostle and High Priest of our
confession") looks back to and summarizes the content of
chapters 1 and 2:

> The compound description (ὁ ἀπόστολος καὶ
> ἀρξιερεύς) gathers up what has been already
> established as to Christ as the last revealer of
> God's will and the fulfiller of man's identity.[8]

> We see, finally, that in the designations applied
> to Christians and the designations applied to
> Christ, all the grand ideas of the two preceding
> chapters are pregnantly summed up.[9]

> Now as "holy brothers, who share in the heav-
> enly calling," we are asked to fix our thoughts
> on Jesus as the apostle, the divine spokesman of
> chapter 1, and also on him as the High Priest
> of chapter 2.[10]

Chapters 1 and 2 also display a vivid juxtaposition of
Christ's deity (1:1—2:4) and humanity (2:5–18). As God,

---

7. Cocksworth, *Holy, Holy, Holy*, 75.

8. Westcott, *Hebrews*, 74.

9. Kendrick, *Hebrews*, 44.

10. Gooding, *An Unshakeable Kingdom*, 107–8.

Jesus is uniquely qualified to be *the* Apostle, the Father's Messenger *par excellence*; and as man, He is qualified to represent man as High Priest before God (2:17; 5:1). As Thomas Torrance has expressed it:

> As Apostle Christ bears witness for God, that He is Holy. As High Priest He acknowledges that witness and says Amen to it. Again as Apostle of God He confesses the mercy and grace of God, His will to pardon and reconcile. As High Priest He intercedes for men, and confesses them before the face of God.[11]

Apostle

Jesus Christ is the first and ultimate[12] Apostle,[13] the climactic and consummate Messenger of God[14] (1:1–2) sent by

11. T. F. Torrance, *Royal Priesthood*, 12.

12. The ultimate and exemplary nature of Christ's role in the Church is beautifully expressed by Saphir: "Of Christ the Head are all energies and ministrations in the body. If there are bishops, it is because Christ is *the* Bishop; if there are pastors or shepherds, it is because Christ is 'the Shepherd of the flock'; if there are evangelists, it is because Christ came and brought to mankind the glad tidings; if there are apostles, it is because He is the Apostle, the head of all apostolic dignity and work. He is the Apostle sent by God to us men" (Saphir, *The Great High Priest,* 170).

13. "The writer of Hebrews talks of no other apostles; he keeps the word for Christ" (Barclay, *Hebrews*, 23).

14. "Now the Word of God is His Son. . . . But He is also called 'Apostle'; for He announces whatever we ought to know, and is sent forth to testify to what is announced, as Our Lord Himself also said: 'He that hears me hears Him who sent me'" (Justin Martyr, *First Apology*, 63); "Christ is designated as the unique, incomparable messenger of God. As one who is sent of God He is the bearer of revelation in the absolute sense" (Schneider, *Hebrews*, 25).

the Father[15] to reveal the divine nature (1:3). As Davies puts it, "The word [apostle] sums up our writer's teaching about the Son coming as God's word into the world."[16] Indeed, speaking and hearing are prominent themes in 1:1—2:4: God has *spoken* to us *by* His Son (1:2); God has *spoken of* His Son (1:5–8); God has *spoken to* His Son (1:13). "We must pay much closer attention to what we have *heard*" (2:1). "The *message declared* by angels proved to be reliable" (2:2). Salvation "was *declared* at first by the Lord" (2:3).[17] And then in 2:12, the writer gives us what he identifies as *the words of Jesus Himself.*

High Priest

The priesthood of Christ, which of course will be much more fully developed later on in the epistle, is first introduced in chapter 2 in the context of discussing His humanity and identification with sinful mankind:

> We see him who for a little while was made lower than the angels, namely Jesus. . . . For he who sanctifies and those who are sanctified all have one origin. That is why he is not ashamed to call them brothers, saying, "I will tell of your name to my brethren . . . ." Since therefore the

15. The term ἀπόστολος has the idea of messenger or emissary, connected with the word's root idea (through ἀποστέλλω) of one who is *sent* (Müller, "Apostle," in *New International Dictionary of New Testament Theology*, 1:26–30). Jesus often described His earthly mission as one of being "sent," especially in John's gospel: e.g., John 3:17; 6:29; 7:29; 8:42; 11:42; 17:3,8,21; 20:21; etc.

16. Davies, *Hebrews*, 34.

17. "The author . . . presents Jesus from the outset as the messenger of God's ultimate word. It was the Son who brought the message and the promises to which the hearers have responded (1:2; 2:3), and who is therefore the preeminent apostle, the one 'sent' from God" (DeSilva, *Perseverance in Gratitude*, 134).

> children share in flesh and blood, he himself likewise partook of the same things. . . . Therefore he had to be made like his brothers in every respect, so that he might become a merciful and faithful high priest in the service of God, to make propitiation for the sins of the people (2:9,11–12,14–17).

It is important to realize that this priesthood, in chapter 2 and 3:1 as well as later, refers not only to Christ's past priestly ministry in offering up Himself as the perfect sacrifice (as some seem to limit the reference in 3:1 to), but also to His continuing priestly role (on which much more will be said later). DeSilva recognizes this fact when he says of 3:1, "Jesus is also 'high priest' in that he represents us to God and maintains the relationship formed with God through Him (2:17; 5:1; 7:25)."[18]

Greater than Moses and Aaron

In 3:1 the author is clearly also looking ahead, where he will demonstrate the superiority of Christ to both Moses (the Old Covenant epitome of the messenger, or apostle, of God; 3:2–6) and Aaron (the first and paradigmatic high priest; chapters 7–10). This has often been observed by commentators.[19]

We will see that the twin roles of Apostle and High Priest are clearly illustrated in microcosm in 2:12.

18. Ibid.

19. Calvin, *Hebrews and the First and Second Epistles of St. Peter*, 77; Bengel, *Gnomon*, 370; Farrar, *Hebrews*, 57; Westcott, *Hebrews*, 74; Lightfoot, *Jesus Christ Today*, 86; Hewitt, *Hebrews*, 77; Brown, *Hebrews*, 154; Vaughan, *Hebrews*, 58.

The Content
of Hebrews 2:12

*"I will proclaim Your name to my brethren, in the
midst of the congregation I will sing Your praise."*
(NASB)

The Words of Jesus

IN HEBREWS 2:12–13 the author quotes from Psalm 22:22
and Isaiah 8:17–18 in demonstration of his point in verse
11 that Jesus identifies Himself with us as brethren.[1] λέγων
introduces these quotations as the words of Jesus Himself.
This is not the only time in his book that the writer of
Hebrews puts Old Testament words on the lips of Jesus: in
10:5–9 he quotes Psalm 40:6–8a as words which Jesus spoke
"when He comes [or came] into the world (εἰσερχόμενος
εἰς τὸν κόσμον)."

---

1. The point of the quotation from Isaiah 8:17 seems to be that
Jesus in His humanity has to trust the Father even as we do. Isaiah
8:18 declares His solidarity with those "children" entrusted to Him
by the Father.

The Quotation from Psalm 22

Psalm 22, identified as a Psalm of David, is usually classified as an "individual lament psalm,"[2] though it is sometimes seen as referring to the national experience of Israel as well.[3]

While discussions continue on the exact nature of the predictive or typological nature of this psalm, it is indisputable that it plays a prominent role in the passion narratives of the gospels.[4] New Testament writers quoting from the Old Testament normally did so with full cognizance and even intentional application of the context from which the quotation was drawn; Bruce makes reference to "C. H. Dodd's thesis that the principal Old Testament quotations in the New Testament are not isolated proof-texts, but carry their contexts with them by association."[5] A number of commentators have identified this principle as being at work in the evangelists' (and Jesus') use of Psalm 22 in the passion narratives: Jesus appropriates to Himself the cry of dereliction of 22:1 (Matt 27:46; Mark 15:34); and the evangelists further draw upon the context of the psalm, by way of quotation and allusion, [6] in other parts of the passion story also.[7]

2. See, for example: Westermann, *Praise and Lament*, 64–65; VanGemeren, *Psalms*, 198.

3. Perowne, *Psalms*, 210–11.

4. See Lange, "The Relationship between Psalm 22 and the Passion Narrative," 610–12.

5. F. F. Bruce, *Hebrews*, 46.

6. The other direct quotation is from 22:18 in John 19:24 (see Archer and Chirichigno, *Old Testament Quotations*, 64–65). Likely allusions include 22:7–8 in Matthew 27:39–43/Mark 15:29; 22:15b in John 19:28; 22:16 in Matthew 27:35/John 20:25; 22:18 in Mark 15:24/Luke 23:34/John 19:24.

7. "As God the Father moulds the history of Jesus Christ in accordance with His own counsel, so His Spirit moulds even the utterances of David concerning himself the type of the Future One, with a view to that history. Through this Spirit, who is the Spirit

The structure of the psalm is commonly seen as a two-

of God and of the future Christ at the same time, David's typical history, as he describes it in the Psalms and more especially in this Psalm, acquires that ideal depth of tone, brilliancy, and power, by virtue of which it (the history) reaches far beyond its typical facts, penetrates to its very root in the divine counsels, and grows to be the word of prophecy: so that, to a certain extent, it may rightly be said that Christ here speaks through David, insofar as the Spirit of Christ speaks through him, and makes the typical suffering of His ancestor the medium for the representation of His own future sufferings" (Delitzsch, *Psalms*, 307).

"Es ist ja von vornherein wahrscheinlich, dass das Zitat des Psalmanfangs den ganzen Psalm meint; denn auch sonst zeigt die Darstellung der Passion einen entscheidenden Einfluss weiterer Stellen dieses Psalmes" ("Indeed, it is from the outset probable that the quotation of the Psalm's beginning [in Matthew 27:46; Mark 15:34] points to the entire Psalm; for elsewhere also the presentation of the Passion shows a decisive influence of other passages of this Psalm.") (Gese, "Psalm 22 und das Neue Testament," 10).

"In the Gospels, Psalm 22 is picked up over and over again, by way of quotation, allusion, or influence, with reference to the death of Jesus and the events surrounding his death, and thus becomes a hermeneutical guide to help us understand what those events mean" (Miller, *Interpreting the Psalms*, 109).

"But it is not just the opening words that are involved. . . . Citing the first words of a text was, in the tradition of the time, a way of identifying an entire passage. Moreover, features of the psalm's description of the psalmist's experience appear in the Gospel narrative. . . . The very experiences of the one who prays in the psalm become part of the scenario of the passion. . . . The canonical relation between passion narrative and psalm invites us also to understand Jesus in terms of the psalm. . . . That would be to follow the example of the apostles and evangelists by using the psalm as a hermeneutical context" (Mays, *Psalms*, 105–6).

"Christ made the lament of Psalm 22 his own lament. How much Jesus himself lived in the Psalms! How much the first Christian community must have lived in the Psalms if it was Psalm 22 in particular which became the Psalm of the passion story!" (Westermann, *Psalms*, 128–29).

All this leads Davidson to conclude that thus "this Psalm is indelibly woven into the fabric of Christian thought and spirituality" part one: lament (vv. 1–21) and thanksgiving (vv. 22–31).[8] Miller says of the second part: "The psalm comes to its conclusion—and one might say in some sense its climax—in one of the most effusive and extravagant songs of thanksgiving in the Old Testament."[9] David's promise to testify of the Lord's greatness to His brethren and to praise Him in their company are the words which Jesus spoke in and through David and appropriates to Himself, according to the author of Hebrews.

It is probably significant that the verse quoted in Hebrews 2:12 is the *first* verse of the second part—certainly suggesting the possibility that the context of all of Psalm 22: 22–31 is in the mind of the writer of Hebrews (similar to how Jesus' use of verse 1 of the Psalm suggests that the entire Psalm is in view). And that context is rich in its Christian implications, as one can see in Mays' statement:

> The setting assumed by the language now is the service of thanksgiving in which a person whose prayer for deliverance has been answered goes to the sanctuary with those who rejoice at his restoration, does what is necessary to keep the vows made in the prayer for help, and provides a sacrificial meal for the company of family and friends who are with him, and sings a song of praise and thanksgiving for his salvation. . . . The group who celebrate his deliverance with him have a theological spiritual identity. They are not simply family, friends, and neighbors, a company constituted by natural and accidental relations. They are brothers (v. 22) in a religious sense. All the different designations refer to this fraternal company:

(Davidson, *The Vitality of Worship*, 78–79).

8. VanGemeren, *Psalms*, 198.

9. Miller, *Interpreting the Psalms*, 107.

"fearers of the LORD" (vv. 23,25); "seekers of the LORD" (v. 26); "the lowly" (v. 26). . . . The company of brothers in faith celebrate not only the salvation of the figure but the good news for them in his deliverance.[10]

Ellingsworth suggests that the repeated references to the death of Christ in the immediate context of Hebrews 2:12 (in 2:9–10, 14–15, 17–18) may have contributed to the author's decision to quote from Psalm 22.[11] And Bruce remarks that seeing Christ in the first half of the Psalm means that "when the psalmist's lament gives way to the public thanksgiving of which the second part of the psalm consists, the same speaker should be recognized, and the once crucified, now exalted Christ should be heard."[12] Westermann adds this intriguing thought: "It is possible that the phrase that appears in Matthew's Easter account, 'go and tell my brethren' (Matt. 28:10) is an allusion to the beginning of the second part of Psalm 22, 'I will tell of thy name to my brethren.'"[13] Kidner cites not only the vivid fulfillment in the crucifixion of Christ of aspects of the suffering described by the Psalmist, but also the sufferer's "vision of a world-wide ingathering of the Gentiles," as evidence of its Messianic referent;[14] certainly the prospect of worldwide praise resulting from the sufferer's deliverance (22:27) goes far beyond David's human expectations![15]

10. Mays, *Psalms*, 111–12.

11. Ellingworth, *Hebrews*, 167.

12. F. F. Bruce, *Hebrews*, 45.

13. Westermann, *Psalms*, 130.

14. Kidner, *Psalms 1–72*, 105.

15. "In Psalm 22 . . . David descends, with his complaint, into a depth that goes beyond the depth of his affliction, and rises, with his hopes, to a height that lies far beyond the height of the reward of his affliction" (Delitzsch, *Psalms*, 308).

Glodo explores the profound implications of Psalm 22 and its complementary motifs of suffering and triumph fulfilled soteriologically in Christ and seen in Hebrews 2:

> The most profound lesson Hebrews 2 teaches us about worship is that, because Jesus sang the first verses of Psalm 22, we don't have to sing them. Instead, we sing the verses of praise with Him. Because he cried out "Abandoned!" we can sing out "Found!" Under the weight of our sin He declared Himself "a worm and not a man" (Ps. 22:6) so that each of us is "no longer a slave but a son" (Gal. 4:7). The frown of God was upon His beloved Son so that divine justice satisfied smiles at us. In worship we sing with our Savior because He first sang for us.[16]

The Time Options

Various views have been espoused as to the point of time which Christ is referring to as regards the proclamation and praise He speaks of in 2:12.

During His Earthly Ministry

A very few commentators, including Lenski and R. H. Smith, have held that 2:12 refers to activities of Jesus during the time of His ministry on earth:

> So Jesus went to the Temple in Jerusalem and sang the psalms of worship among his brother worshipers.[17]

16. Glodo, "Singing with the Savior."
17. Lenski, *Hebrews and the Epistle of James*, 86.

This looks like a reference to the work of Jesus in the days of his ministry, when he declared the message of salvation (2:3) by which he revealed the name or reality of God.[18]

At the Consummation

Others think that the reference is solely to the time of the future consummation, for instance Newell: "It is the *glorified* saints whom Christ is leading in praise."[19] Lane also holds this view:

> The writer to the Hebrews locates here a reference to the exalted Lord who finds in the gathering of the people of God at the parousia an occasion for the proclamation of God's name and who as the singing priest leads the redeemed community . . . in songs of praise.[20]

Some holding this view point out that the only other use of ἐκκλησία in the book of Hebrews is found in 12:23, where, they maintain, the reference is only to the glorified saints at the consummation. But the consummation is clearly not in view solely, because the context states that the readers "*have* come" (προσεληλύθατε) to this heavenly assembly; therefore their present state must be involved. Ellingworth observes: "Even in 12:23, the worship of the ἐκκλησία πρωτοτόκων in the heavenly Jerusalem is a liturgy in which the readers participate (προσεληλύθατε)."[21]

Poythress makes another salient argument against this view:

18. Smith, *Hebrews*, 49.

19. Newell, *Hebrews*, 55.

20. Lane, *Hebrews 1–8*, 58.

21. Ellingworth, *Hebrews*, 168.

The author's main reason for introducing the quotation in Heb. 2:12 is to confirm his point that Christ calls his people brothers (2:10–11). His argument is seriously weakened if Ps. 22:22 applies only to the consummation, because then, for all we know, it may be only at the consummation that Christ is willing to call men brothers. Clearly the author of Hebrews feels justified in assuming that Christ is *now* willing to use such words as Ps. 22:22.[22]

In The Church

Exegetically and contextually the best view is that 2:12 is referring to Jesus' continuing ministry during the Church Age. This view has been variously and convincingly defended:

Quite apart from quotations and allusions to Ps. 22 in the Gospel passion narratives, the reference in Ps. 22:30f. to a "coming generation" and a "people yet to be born" may have impressed the author of Hebrews as pointing towards fulfilment in Christ and in his Church. If so, this fact may have contributed to his decision to quote v. 22b (LXX 23b) as referring to the Church. It also suggests that the time perspective of the quotations in Heb. 2:12f. is that of realized eschatology. . . . From the time of Christ's exaltation and the establishment of the Christian ἐκκλησία, the future tenses in the quotations, though still quoted as such, have become present reality.[23]

---

22. Poythress, "Ezra 3," 85.

23. Ellingworth, *Hebrews*, 168.

The employment of this word [ἐκκλησία] in synonymous parallelism with "brethren" in a Christian context indicates that those whom the Son of God is pleased to call His brethren are the members of His church.[24]

The author's main reason for introducing the quotation in Hebrews 2:12 is to confirm his point that Christ calls His people brothers (2:10–11). . . . Clearly the author of Hebrews feels justified in assuming that Christ is *now* willing to use such words as Psalm 22:22.[25]

The "present-tense" interpretation of Ps. 22:22 is confirmed by the context of Ps. 22. The purpose of proclamation to the brethren is that the message of salvation and the worship of God may spread to all the earth (22:25–31). Hence Ps. 22:22 is in a pre-consummation setting.[26]

Vocabulary

The only difference between the text of the LXX in Psalm 22:22 and the citation in Hebrews 2:12 is the writer's use of the verb ἀπαγγέλλω in place of διηγέομαι. The choice of verb may be for the purposes of adding an alliterative connection to the conceptual link with ἀπόστολος in 3:1;

24. Bruce, *Hebrews*, 46. The use of ἐκκλησία here is not conclusive, since the author is simply quoting from the LXX; but the use is at least suggestive, and the author may well have had the New Testament understanding of the word in mind as one reason for using Psalm 22:22.

25. Poythress, "Ezra 3," 85.

26. Ibid., 85.

less likely is a linguistic tie to the angels referred to repeatedly in chapters 1 and 2.

The author's choice of a LXX text using the term ἐκκλησία may be a deliberate move to highlight the word's new identification with Christ's "brethren," the New Covenant people of God.

3

The Significance
of Hebrews 2:12

Hebrews 2:12 encapsulates two continuing and complementary post-ascension activities of Christ, with many implications for a richer and more biblical view of preaching and corporate worship.

Proclamation (2:12a)

"I will proclaim Your name to my brethren,"

The Passage

Jesus is addressing His Father in both halves of 2:12. In the first clause we see His intention to proclaim the Father's Name, that is, His nature, to those whom He is not ashamed to call His brethren (2:11).

This is consonant with much which we have already seen in the context. As earlier mentioned, there is an emphasis in chapters 1 and 2 on hearing the message of God: as proclaimed through His Old Testament messengers (1:2); climactically, definitively and supremely through His Son (1:2; 2:3b); and through those whom He delegates to carry on this communication (2:3b). Jesus' status as God's ultimate Messenger is also suggested by his appellation as "the Apostle . . . of our confession" in 3:1.

In addition, it should be remembered, especially in light of 3:1 and the following contrast with Moses (who was the supreme Old Testament messenger of God), that Peter in Acts 3:22 claims that Jesus is the ultimate fulfillment of the "prophet like Moses" promised in Deuteronomy 18:

> [Moses said,] The Lord your God will raise up for you a prophet like me from among you, from your brothers—it is to him you shall listen. . . . [God said,] "I will raise up for them a prophet like you from among their brothers. And I will put my words in his mouth, and he shall speak to them all that I command him" (Deut 18:15, 18).

Jesus, the prophet like Moses, came as God's spokesman, and hence must be listened to.

Thus Acts 3:22 hints at His role as proclaimer and redeemer, which is then so succinctly stated in Hebrews 2:12:

> Here the Son is heard addressing the Father, promising that He would execute the charge which had been given Him. The Greek word for "declare" is very emphatic and comprehensive. It means, To proclaim and publish, to exhibit and make known. To declare God's "Name" signifies to reveal what God is, to make known His excellencies and counsels. This is what Christ came here to do: see John 17:6, 26. None else was competent for such a task, for none knoweth the Father but the Son (Matt. 11:27).[1]

Other Passages and Insights

There are a host of other Scriptures which speak to the issue of Christ's revelatory ministry, past and present; and

1. Pink, *Hebrews*, 122.

commentators and theologians have given insights into this subject as well.

JESUS' EARTHLY MISSION

A great many passages from the gospels make it clear that Jesus' mission while on earth was to deliver God's message and reveal the Father.[2]

2. "'All things have been handed over to me by my Father, and no one knows the Son except the Father, and no one knows the Father except the Son and anyone to whom the Son chooses to reveal him'" (Matt. 11:27). "'The one who listens to you listens to Me, and the one who rejects you rejects Me; and he who rejects Me rejects the One who sent Me'" (Luke 10:16). "No one has seen God at any time; the only begotten God who is in the bosom of the Father, He has explained Him" (John 1:18). "'He bears witness to what he has seen and heard, yet no one receives his testimony. . . . For he whom God has sent utters the words of God, for he gives the Spirit without measure. The Father loves the Son and has given all things into his hand'" (John 3:32, 34–35). "So Jesus said to them, 'Truly, truly, I say to you, the Son can do nothing of his own accord, but only what he sees the Father doing. For whatever the Father does, that the Son does likewise. For the Father loves the Son and shows him all that he himself is doing. And greater works than these will he show him, so that you may marvel'" (John 5:19–20). "So Jesus answered them, 'My teaching is not mine, but his who sent me'" (John 7:16). "They said to him therefore, 'Where is your Father?' Jesus answered, 'You know neither me nor my Father. If you knew me, you would know my Father also'" (John 8:19). "'I have much to say about you and much to judge, but he who sent me is true, and I declare to the world what I have heard from him.' They did not understand that he had been speaking to them about the Father. So Jesus said to them, 'When you have lifted up the Son of Man, then you will know that I am he, and that I do nothing on my own authority, but speak just as the Father taught me'" (John 8:26–28). "'I speak of what I have seen with my Father'" (John 8:38a). "'For I have not spoken on my own authority, but the Father who sent me has himself given me a commandment— what to say and what to speak. And I know that his commandment is eternal life. What I say, therefore, I say as the Father has told me'" (John 12:49–50). "'If you had known me, you would have known

JESUS' CONTINUING MINISTRY OF REVELATION

There are also a number of Scriptures which speak of or imply the continuation of Jesus' ministry of revealing the Father *after* His glorification.

One remarkable passage along these lines is found in the Messianic Psalm 40, verses 6–8a of which figure so prominently in Hebrews 10. In the verses of Psalm 40 *immediately following* those quoted in Hebrews 10:5–9, we read:

> I have *told* the glad news of deliverance in the great congregation; behold, I have *not restrained my lips*, as you know, O Lord. I have *not hidden* your deliverance within my heart; I have *spoken* of your faithfulness and your salvation; I have *not concealed* your steadfast love and your faithfulness from the great congregation (Ps 40: 9–10).

---

my Father also. From now on you do know him and have seen him.' Philip said to him, 'Lord, show us the Father, and it is enough for us.' Jesus said to him, 'Have I been with you so long, and you still do not know me, Philip? Whoever has seen me has seen the Father. How can you say, "Show us the Father"?'" (John 14:7–9). "'No longer do I call you servants, for the servant does not know what his master is doing; but I have called you friends, for all that I have heard from my Father I have made known to you'" (John 15:15). "'Glorify your Son that the Son may glorify you, since you have given him authority over all flesh, to give eternal life to all whom you have given him. And this is eternal life, that they know you the only true God, and Jesus Christ whom you have sent. I glorified you on earth, having accomplished the work that you gave me to do'" (John 17:1c–4). "'I have manifested Your name to the men whom You gave Me out of the world; now they know that everything that you have given me is from you. For I have given them the words that you gave me, and they have received them and have come to know in truth that I came from you; and they have believed that you sent me'" (John 17:6–8). "'I have given them your word'" (John 17:14a). "'O righteous Father, even though the world does not know you, I know you, and these know that you have sent me. I made known to them your name'" (John 17:25–26a).

The writer of Hebrews explicitly tells us that Psalm 40:6–8a are the words of Jesus Himself, so it is only natural to regard the following verses that way as well. There he repeatedly shows His intention (in past tense, prophetically) to proclaim God's nature and deliverance to the "congregation."[3]

A number of other New Testament passages further highlight the idea of Christ's continuing ministry of revelation:

1. In Matthew 11:27, Jesus says, "All things have been handed over to Me by My Father; and no one knows the Son except the Father; nor does anyone know the Father except the Son, and anyone to whom the Son wills to reveal Him." There is no reason to think, especially in light of the other evidence, that this does not have continuing validity.

2. Speaking on the evening before His crucifixion, Jesus speaks of the coming ministry of the Spirit as one of continuing Jesus' revelatory ministry:

> I still have many things to say to you, but you cannot bear them now. When the Spirit of truth comes, he will guide you into all the truth, for he will not speak on his own authority, but whatever he hears he will speak, and he will declare to you the things that are to come. He will glorify me, for he will take what is mine and declare it to you. All that the Father has is mine; therefore I said that he will take what is mine and declare it to you (John 16:12–15).

3. The term קָהֵל is used in both verse 9 and 10, and is translated by the LXX as συναγωγή in verse 10 (LXX 39:11), but as ἐκκλησία in verse 9 (LXX 39:10)! Once again it is intriguing to see how the author of Hebrews chooses an LXX text which includes ἐκκλησία and identifies the words as being Christ's (as with Psalm 22:22/Hebrews 2:12); and there is also here a striking similarity of theme with Hebrews 2:12a.

3. Jesus is certainly looking past the cross when he says in John 16:25: "I have said these things to you in figures of speech. *The hour is coming* when I will no longer speak to you in figures of speech but will tell you plainly about the Father."

4. On the same evening He also said in His prayer to the Father, "I have made Your name known to them, and *will make it known*" (John 17:26).

5. Luke begins the sequel to his gospel by writing, "The first account I composed, Theophilus, about all that Jesus *began* to do and teach . . ." (Acts 1:1). The book of Acts is intended to be Luke's account of what Jesus *continued* "to do and teach."

6. The question πῶς δὲ πιστεύσωσιν οὗ οὐκ ἤ-κουσαν in Romans 10:14 should properly be translated as it is in the NASB, "How will they believe in Him *whom* they have not heard?"[4] As Morris puts it, "The point is that

---

4. A great number of translations, however, from the AV to the ESV (and including the NJB, NAB, RSV, NIV and NLT) obscure the correct meaning when they translate it as, "How are they to believe in him *of whom* they have never heard?" (ESV). Blass/Debrunner/Funk observe that the normal Greek usage with the verb ἀκούειν is: "the person whose words are heard stands in the genitive, the thing (or person . . .) about which (or whom) one hears in the accusative" (*A Greek Grammar*, 95 #173). According to this rule, since the genitive is used in 10:14, the correct translation is "whom" and not "of whom." Surprisingly, Bauer/Arndt/Gingrich/Danker seem to side with the translations rather than the grammar, in citing this text as an example of ἀκούω "with the genitive of the person"; however, circular reasoning seems to be at work, as Romans 10:14 is the *only* text cited as an example of such a genitive use with that verb! (*A Greek-English Lexicon*, 32).

Many commentators, on the other hand, in spite of the translations acknowledge the clear implication of the grammatical construction in its normal usage, and prefer the translation "whom" rather than "of whom": so Barrett, *Romans*, 204; Cranfield, *Romans*, 534; Morris,

Christ is present in the preachers; to hear them is to hear him."[5] Barrett similarly states, "Christ must be heard either in his own person, or in the person of his preachers, through whom his own word (v. 17) is spoken; otherwise faith in him is impossible."[6] For Cranfield, too, "the thought is of their hearing Christ speaking in the message of the preachers."[7] Christ is still speaking through the agency of servants who faithfully proclaim his message.

7. We find a continuation of the same idea in Romans 10:17: "So faith comes from hearing, and hearing through the word of Christ [διὰ ῥήματος χριστοῦ]." Grammatically χριστοῦ can be taken as either a subjective genitive ("the word *about Christ*") or an objective genitive ("the word *of* or *from Christ*"—"i.e., through Christ's speaking the message by the mouths of his messengers"[8]). Because of the proximity and connection with verse 14 (a connection observed by Cranfield[9] and Barrett[10]), it is probably better to see this as a subjective genitive; however, Morris prefers to see a double meaning of the genitive at play here:

> It is possible to understand this expression either as referring to the teaching of the historical Jesus passed on in the church or to the teaching of the exalted Lord, the Lord of the church.

Romans, 390; Murray, *Romans*, 58.

5. Morris, *Romans*, 390.

6. Barrett, *Romans*, 204.

7. Cranfield, *Romans*, 534.

8. Ibid., 537.

9. Ibid.

10. Barrett, *Romans*, 205.

> Probably it is both, for there seems no reason
> for separating the two.[11]

Regardless of which conclusion is drawn on the genitive construction, Morris' conclusion holds true and is well taken:

> Whether we take this to mean "the word about Christ" or "the word from Christ," it locates the content of the preaching in what God has given, not in what the preacher has thought up.[12]

8. A similar construction is found in Colossians 3:16: "Let the word of Christ [ὁ λόγος τοῦ χριστοῦ] richly dwell within you, with all wisdom teaching and admonishing one another with psalms and hymns and spiritual songs, singing with thankfulness in your hearts to God." In this case commentators are more divided over whether τοῦ χριστοῦ is a subjective or an objective genitive. Bruce[13] and Lightfoot[14] see a subjective genitive; their case may be strengthened by the fact that, unlike the common ὁ λόγος τοῦ θεοῦ, the phrase here is the only occurrence in the New Testament and may be seen as parallel in meaning to ῥήματος χριστοῦ in Romans 10:17; though O'Brien sides with the objective genitive, he allows that the subjective reading is possible and would suggest "that Christ himself is the speaker when his word is proclaimed."[15] Interestingly, the New Living Translation renders the second clause of 3:16: "Use his words to teach and counsel each other."

---

11. Morris, *Romans*, 392.

12. Ibid.

13. Simpson and F. Bruce, *Ephesians and Colossians*, 283.

14. Lightfoot, *Colossians and Philemon*, 224.

15. O'Brien, *Colossians, Philemon*, 206.

John Murray offers the following supporting observations about the continuing revelatory ministry of Jesus in the Church:

> The Gospel, in distinction from the Acts, is concerned with what Jesus began to do and teach. So what Luke records in the present treatise is what Jesus *continued* to do and teach. The Gospel of Luke closes with the ascension of Christ into heaven; the book of Acts is therefore concerned with the doing of teaching of Christ from his exalted glory. . . . Prejudice is done to the work of Christ and to our faith in him when we overlook or even fail to emphasize the continued ministry of Christ in both doing and teaching. He is ever active in the exercise of his prophetic, priestly, and kingly offices.[16]

16. Murray, "The Living Saviour," 40–41. He goes on to add: "The fact that Jesus continued to teach after his ascension is of paramount importance for the authority of Christ in the teaching of the apostles and in the books of the New Testament. Prior to his ascension Christ's teaching was directly by word of mouth. But afterwards he taught by a different mode. He taught by the ministry of appointed witnesses and inspired writers. The New Testament, all of which was written after Jesus' ascension, is not one whit less the teaching of our Lord than that delivered verbally during the days of his flesh. How utterly false it is to set up a contrast between the authority of Jesus' spoken words and the authority of the New Testament as Scripture. The latter is the teaching of Christ given in his own appointed way after his ascension.

"We are reminded of Jesus' word to the disciples: 'I have yet many things to say unto you, but ye cannot bear them now. Howbeit when he, the Spirit of truth, is come he will guide you into all truth' (John 16:12,13). It is from his own lips the certification of Luke's statement in our text. The guiding of the Holy Spirit into all truth does not suspend Jesus' own speaking. 'I have yet many things to say unto you.' But he says these things through the Holy Spirit and thus there is the seal of both divine persons, the Son and the Spirit. Let us prize with the ardour of our whole soul what Jesus continues to do, and teach. He is the living, acting, and teaching Lord."

William Tait, after reminding us that the risen Lord taught His disciples during the forty days leading up to ascension (as Acts 1:3 makes clear), adds this insight:

> Nor did his ascension put a period to this blessed work: he has been engaged in it ever since, and is engaged in it still. All who in any generation, have known the Father's name, and all who know it now, have learnt it from his teaching. None else is competent to teach it. For "no man," Jesus himself declares, "knoweth the Father save the Son, and he to whomsoever the Son will reveal him" (Matt. 11:27). This blessed work is Christ's delight, my brethren. . . . The invisible Father shall never be known save in and through the Son; and therefore as Jesus shall delight to teach, his people shall delight to learn of him.[17]

JESUS SPEAKING THROUGH HIS WORD AND BY HIS SERVANTS

Obviously the way Jesus speaks to us of the Father's glory is different now than the way He did so during His earthly ministry. Owen identifies the contrast:

> There are two ways whereby the Lord Christ declared this name of God: (1) In *his own person*; and that both before and after his sufferings. . . . Thus in the days of his flesh, he instructed his disciples and preached the gospel in the synagogues of the Jews and in the temple, declaring the name of God unto them. So also after his resurrection he conferred with his apostles about the kingdom of God, Acts 1. (2) By *his Spirit*; and both in the effusion of it upon his disciples, enabling them personally to preach the gospel

17. Tait, *Meditationes Hebraicae*, 160–61.

unto the men of their own generation, and in the
inspiration of some of them, enabling them to
commit the truth unto writing for the instruc-
tion of the elect unto the end of the world.[18]

Now Jesus works through the appointed means of
the Scriptures (inspired by the Holy Spirit, whom He sent
to teach the apostles and bring to their remembrance the
things He had said, John 14:26) and through the gifted
preachers and teachers He gives to the Church (Eph 4:11–
13). He continues to speak through His chosen means and
spokesmen: "The one who listens to you listens to Me, and
the one who rejects you rejects Me; and he who rejects Me
rejects the One who sent Me" (Luke 10:16).

Christ's ministry of proclaiming the Father's name to
His brethren (Hebrews 2:12a) is incarnated in the Church's
worship as the Word is set forth in its various ways.[19] It is
crucial to remember that it is *His* ministry, ever and always,
to reveal to us the Father (Matt 11:27). He is God's final
word, *and* He has the final word about God (Heb 1:2).

And this is of course the great thing about true
preaching among the people of God in the
power of the Holy Spirit—that whoever does
the preaching is incidental to the One who is
truly preaching: our Lord Jesus Christ.[20]

We must further notice the office which Christ
assumes, which is that of *proclaiming the name*

18. Owen, *Hebrews*, 425.

19. "The Lord Christ, in his own person, by his Spirit in his
apostles, by his word, and by all his messengers unto the end of the
world, [sets] forth the love, grace, goodness, and mercy of God" (Ibid.,
426). "In Scripture reading and sermon, in sacrament and in liturgical
action, Christ proclaims God to man" (Nicholls, *Jacob's Ladder*, 38).

20. Ferguson, "True Spirituality, True Worship."

of God; and this began to be done when the gospel was first promulgated, and is now done daily by the ministry of pastors.[21]

Christ is the author of the gospel in whatever manner it may be offered to us. And this is what Paul says, for he declares that he and others were ambassadors for Christ; and he exhorted men as it were in the name of Christ (2 Cor. 5:20). And this ought to add no small reverence to the gospel, since we ought not so much to consider men as speaking to us, as Christ by his own mouth.[22]

We should not conclude from all the above that the canon is open, that sermons preached and lessons taught add authoritative new revelation from Christ to His Church. Rather, the point is: to the extent that the truth of God is reliably proclaimed and communicated through his servants, it is as a result of the ministry of the living Christ speaking by his Spirit in and through those servants. The truth communicated is God's truth; Christ is the mediator of that truth; and preachers and teachers of the Word are the conduits through which Christ by his Spirit conveys and illuminates that truth. That should certainly affect the attitude with which we preach and teach, *and* the attitude with which we listen!

---

21. Calvin, *Commentaries on the Epistle to the Hebrews*, 66.
22. Ibid.

Praise (2:12b)

". . . in the midst of the congregation I will sing your praise."

The Passage

The second half of 2:12 contains the complementary thought that the speaker will also sing the Father's praise in the assembled congregation. There are ample reasons to see v. 12b as fulfilled by Jesus in the gathering of the church, as we have seen v. 12a also to be: (1) the use of ἐκκλησία at least suggests that the writer of Hebrews has the assembly of the church in view (in other words, the appearance of this word may not be simply happenstance in a quotation chosen for other reasons); (2) this probability is heightened by the term "brethren" in v. 12a, which is parallel to ἐκκλησία in 12b—the whole point of the quotation is to demonstrate Christ's identification with his people, i.e. "those who are sanctified" (v. 11) by his suffering (vv. 9–10), i.e., the church; (3) this view is consistent with the context of the second part of Psalm 22, which sees the victorious sufferer proclaiming and praising God in the company of his brethren.

A couple of questions arise from this interpretation:

To Whom Is Christ Singing?

Poythress and others appear to see in Psalm 22:22 (and its quotation in Hebrews 2:12) a *synonymous* parallelism, so that Hebrews 2:12b is saying pretty much the same thing as 2:12a: "Hebrews 2:12 pictures Christ as singing *to the congregation* the account of the eschatological deliverance of God's chosen One."[23] In other words, both 12a and 12b

---

23. Poythress, "Ezra 3," 85 (emphasis mine). Poythress seems to contradict himself when he later writes: "Christ sings *to* the Lord God *among* the congregation" (Poythress, "Ezra 3 [Concluded]," 222). But

are held to be Christ's communication about God to his people, a downward movement in both instances—Christ proclaiming His name in verse 12a and proclaiming His praiseworthiness in verse 12b.

However, it is better to see in this verse a *synthetic* parallelism, with the two halves regarded as complementary but *in opposite directions*: "I will declare your name to my brethren [downward, God to man], and in the midst of the congregation I will sing Your praise [upward, man to God]." This view is supported by the biblical usage of the verb used in the LXX of Psalm 22:22 and in Hebrews 2:12b, ὑμνέω,[24] and its correspondent Hebrew term in Psalm 22:22, הָלַל.[25] The consistent usage of both terms is that when they take an object, it is God who is the recipient. Various English translations concur that *God* is the one who is being sung *to* (not just *about*) in Hebrews 2:12 (e.g., KJV, RSV, ESV, NASB, NIV, NLT, RSV).

For these reasons, it is best to interpret the two halves of Hebrews 2:12 as referring to two quite distinct, though marvelously complementary, activities: the declaration of God's praiseworthiness to the people (12a), and the appropriate praise then lifted to God in response (12b).

Is Christ Leading the People's Praise?

Another question concerns the corollary concept, which is assumed though not really defended by a number of com-

---

in that context he is also dealing with Ephesians 5:19 and Colossians 3:16, pointing out that singing in those verses is explicitly directed *both* to people and to God.

24. See in the LXX: Judg 16:24; 1 Chr 16:10; 2 Chr 29:30; Isa 12:4,5; 25:1; 42:10; and in the NT: Acts 16:25.

25. See, for example, in the Hebrew Bible: Jdg 16:24; 2 Sam 22:4; 1 Chr 16:4,10; 2 Chr 5:13; Ezra 3:10; Neh 5:13; Ps 18:4; 22:24; 96:4; 150:1–6.

mentators,[26] that Jesus' praise of the Father in the midst of the assembly constitutes *leading* His people as well in their praises. This is an indeed an important concept for understanding the Christological dynamic of New Testament worship. While it is not directly stated in Hebrews 2:12, it may be inferred from the following:

1.   Already we have considered the probable relevance of the context of Psalm 22:22 in the mind of the writer of Hebrews as he makes his quotation; and indeed much of the second section of Psalm 22 consists of a call by the vindicated one to His brethren to join in with Him in praise to God.[27] That includes the very next verse after the one quoted: "You who fear the LORD, praise Him; All you descendants of Jacob, glorify Him, And stand in awe of Him, all you descendants of Israel" (22:23). Certainly the one praising God in 22:22 (and the one quoted in Hebrews 2:12) intends to draw others into praise with Him!

2.   The immediate reason for the writer of Hebrews to quote Psalm 22:22 (and the following verses from Isaiah 8) is to demonstrate Christ's solidarity with us, His brethren (Hebrews 2:11–13). It is only natural that we should follow our "forerunner" (6:20) and the "author and perfecter of [our] faith" (12:2) as He praises the Father.

26.   E.g., Calvin, *Hebrews and the First and Second Epistles of St. Peter*, 27; James B. Torrance, *Worship, Community and the Triune God of Grace*, 17, 88–89; Ferguson, "True Spirituality, True Worship."

27.   "His . . . response is to say to God that he will offer him praise in that same congregation. Thus, the praise of God that follows is not addressed to God in a vacuum; it is addressed to God through the congregation, with the invitation that they too honor and praise God. The psalmist's invitation to the congregation . . . is taken up in vv. 28–32, where the whole congregation joins in the praise" (Craigie, *Psalms 1–50*, 201).

3. Christ is seen to be the enabler of our worship in Hebrews 7:25: "Therefore He is able also to save forever those who draw near to God *through Him*." προσέρξομαι ("draw near") is a common LXX word for drawing near to God in worship.[28]

4. The priesthood of Christ is a major theme in Hebrews; and one crucial activity of a priest is *leading the people in worship*. (See the discussion later of Christ's similarity to Aaron in the Godward response of worship, in the section "The Two-Way Mediation of Christ," pp. 48–51 below.)

a) The writer asserts in 8:1–2 our great High Priest "has taken His seat at the right hand of the throne of the Majesty in the heavens," where He serves as "a minister" (λειτουργός) in the sanctuary and in the true tabernacle." In the LXX λειτουργέω and its cognates "are used almost exclusively for the service of priests and Levites in the temple."[29] As our connection, our bridge, our "Jacob's Ladder" between earth and heaven, Christ leads us in praise in our midst and transports us spiritually to the heavenly tabernacle to commune with the Father in Him.[30]

28. W. Mundle, "Come," *New International Dictionary of New Testament Theology*, 1:322. Schierse sees our access to God through Christ's present priestly ministry as foundational to a proper understanding of the entire book of Hebrews: "God's only-begotten Son and his adopted sons are brothers from all eternity. Underlying these mysterious words, with all that they imply, we catch a glimpse of the basic idea of the whole letter—the faithful as a liturgical community which approaches God's throne under the leadership of Jesus its high priest" (Schierse, *Hebrews*, 12).

29. K. Hess, "Serve," *New International Dictionary of New Testament Theology*, 3:551.

30. Ferguson comments on 8:2: "He has gathered us into a new assembly in which the Lord Jesus Christ is a 'minister in the holy places. . . .' Jesus is the λειτουργός, He is the Liturgist, He is the Worship Leader in that heavenly sanctuary; so that when we 'go to church' in the power of the Spirit, we go to the church where the

b) It stands to reason that our Priest is the one who must lead us in offering our sacrifice, which is now identified as a "sacrifice of praise" (13:15); and this verse explicitly states that we make that sacrifice "through Him."

c) Jesus' role as the "High Priest of our confession" (3:1) is not limited to His past priestly work accomplished in His atoning sacrifice (as we have seen in 2:12a that neither was His role as Apostle/Messenger/Revealer limited to His pre-cross ministry). The writer of Hebrews hints at the past and present aspects of Christ's priestly work in 2:17 and 2:18 respectively; and he will do so again so later, and with more direct reference to worship, when in turning to make application in 10:19-22 of the great truths he has been expounding in the epistle up until that point, he refers to both Christ's *past* priestly work in 10:19–20 and his *present* priestly work as our "great priest over the house of God" in 10:21.

d) Furthermore, Hebrews 10:19–25 speaks of our free access into the presence of God through Christ, as well as the importance of our assembling together. Quite likely there is a connection and corporate worship, enabled and led by Christ, is in view.

e) Murray concurs that the continuing priestly ministry of Christ has a Godward trajectory:

> It was in pursuance of his priestly office that Christ offered himself a sacrifice to God upon the cross. . . . But that he does not discontinue

---

Lord Jesus is the minister, where the Lord Jesus is the Leader of His people's worship. When the author of Hebrews says this, he is picking up one of the strands of what he has already been saying in Hebrews 2 about the kind of ministry that the Lord Jesus has to His people as His people's High Priest [2:12]—because we have this kind of High Priest, he says, as we engage in worship we are led into presence of God by our Worship Leader, our Lord Jesus Christ" (Ferguson, "True Spirituality, True Worship").

his priestly office and function is equally patent.
. . . His specifically high priestly ministrations
are more operative and pervasive in the church
upon earth than we are frequently disposed to
appreciate. . . . His continued activity has a
Godward reference as truly as did his finished
priestly offering.[31]

5. In the broader context of the New Testament, we
see the clear teaching of our *union with Christ* (1 Cor 1:30;
Eph 2:7,10,13; 2 Tim 1:7; 1 Pet 5:14; among many other
passages). And being in union with Him, we naturally follow Him as our example, model, substitute, and way to the
Father; and so we follow Him into the Father's presence and
add our praises to His own. Indeed, Hebrews 2:12b helps
to elucidate the fuller meaning of the many scriptural references which state that our worship is *through Christ*.[32]

31. Murray, "The Heavenly, Priestly Activity of Christ," 44–47.
32. "First, I thank my God through Jesus Christ for you all,
because your faith is being proclaimed throughout the whole world"
(Rom 1:8). "And not only this, but we also exult in God through
our Lord Jesus Christ, through whom we have now received the
reconciliation" (Rom 5:11). "Thanks be to God through Jesus Christ
our Lord! (Rom 7:25). "To the only wise God, through Jesus Christ, be
the glory forever. Amen" (Rom 16:27). "For as many as are the promises
of God, in Him they are yes; therefore also through Him is our Amen to
the glory of God through us" (2 Cor 1:20). "For through Him we both
have our access in one Spirit to the Father" (Eph 2:18). "Whatever you
do in word or deed, do all in the name of the Lord Jesus, giving thanks
through Him to God the Father" (Col 3:17). "Therefore He is able
also to save forever those who draw near to God through Him, since
He always lives to make intercession for them" (Heb 7:25). "Through
Him then, let us continually offer up a sacrifice of praise to God, that
is, the fruit of lips that give thanks to His name" (Heb 13:15). "You
also, as living stones, are being built up as a spiritual house for a holy
priesthood, to offer up spiritual sacrifices acceptable to God through
Jesus Christ" (1 Pet 2:5). "To the only God our Savior, through Jesus
Christ our Lord, be glory, majesty, dominion and authority, before all

It is a natural conclusion that our praises would be in conjunction with, motivated by, empowered by, even led by, Christ's praises "in the midst of the assembly" (Hebrews 2:12b): He enables and empowers His brethren's response to the truth which He has also been the effectual Agent in bringing to them (2:12a). When He sings the Father's praises in the midst of the assembly, He is not singing a solo! Rather He leads us in our praises. When Christ our Model and Brother praises the Father, He leads the way and shows the way for us. Because we are in union with Him, His worship is our worship. We come in and through Him into the Father's presence in worship; we come clothed in His righteousness, and He bears up our weak offerings of worship and makes them one with His own perfect offering of praise. "The real agent in all true worship is Jesus Christ."[33] "Whatever else our worship is, it is our liturgical amen to the worship of Christ."[34] He is not an observer—He is the Leader of our worship. While Hebrews 2:12 does not state this explicitly, it is a logical corollary to what 12b says, in the light of the immediate context, the context of Hebrews, and the context of the entire New Testament.

Christ is, in Calvin's words, "the chief Conductor of our hymns"![35] Vaughan writes:

> The second clause of the quotation introduces a new particular. *The glorified Saviour is not only the Church's brother, revealing to it the Father; He is also the Church's precentor, leading its wor-*

---

time and now and forever. Amen" (Jude 25).

33. James B. Torrance, *Worship, Community and the Triune God of Grace*, 17.

34. Ibid., 14.

35. Calvin, *Hebrews and the First and Second Epistles of St. Peter*, 27.

ship. So entire is the unity between Christ and His
people, as set forth in prophetic Scripture.[36]

Worshiped and Worshiper

"A priest not worshipping, is indeed a contradiction. And
God hath sworn and will not repent that Jesus is a Priest
forever."[37]

We can only marvel at the inscrutability of the
Incarnation when faced with the fact that this One who is
worthy of our worship Himself offers worship to the Father:

> Here lies the mystery, the wonder, the glory of
> the Gospel, that He who is God, the Creator

36. Vaughan, *Hebrews*, 45 (italics are Vaughan's). Along those
same lines, it is interesting to note that the superscription of Psalm 22
is "to the choirmaster"!

37. Tait, *Meditationes Hebraicae*, 164. This is one of at least three
lines of argument against the view of some that the present glorified
state of Christ precludes the possibility of Him offering worship to
the Father. As Tait points out: (1) *A priest who leads worship must
himself be a worshiper.* True and full mediation must certainly include
this aspect.

To this may added:

(2) Jesus may continue as a worshiper on account of *His continuing
full humanity* (see pages 37–41); in heaven we will likewise be
worshipers in our glorified humanity.

(3) *The eternal subordination of the Son to the Father* (1 Cor 3:23;
11:3; 15:24,28; Phil 2:10–11) would seem to allow for a bearing of
worship in this relationship, now as during Jesus' earthly sojourn.
(See Korvach and Schemm, "A Defense of the Doctrine of the Eternal
Subordination of the Son," *JETS* 42 [1999]:461–76). It is interesting
to note that Sinclair Ferguson suggests that there is a hint of this
subordination even in the glorious heavenly scene in Revelation 5; he
bases this on the fact that the Father is seen to be sitting on the throne,
while the Son is (suggesting a mediatorial position) "standing between
the throne and the four living creatures and among the elders" (Rev 5:6
ESV) (Ferguson, "The Church's Worship").

of all things, and worthy of the worship and
praises of all creation, should become man and
as a man worship God, and as a man lead us in
our worship of God, that we might become the
sons of God we are meant to be.[38]

Christ has not only opened they way into the Father's
presence, He not only shows us the way, but He also actively
leads us in our worship and *leads* us to the throne of God:

And because he is our priest, and because we
are invited to receive his priestly ministry for
us and to be included in his holy humanity,
our worship is a participation in his worship.
Christ is the 'minister of the new sanctuary,'
the leader of our worship. He proclaims God
and praises God 'in the midst of the congregation' (2:12). . . . He calls us to join his voice
and to share in his song.[39]

---

38. James B. Torrance, "The Place of Jesus Christ in Worship,"
351.

39. Cocksworth, *Holy, Holy, Holy*, 159. Likewise Peter Toon: "The
church on earth is united in the Holy Spirit with the Lord Jesus Christ,
Son of the Father, and High Priest in heaven: her worship ascends to
the Father within the worship and prayer offered unceasingly by Jesus
to the Father" (Toon, *Our Triune God*, 224).

4

Contiguous
New Testament Themes

THE ABOVE understanding of Hebrews 2:12 enhances and enriches a number of important New Testament concepts.

The Continuing Humanity and Priesthood of Christ

Jesus Christ in His incarnation was "made for a little while lower than the angels" (Heb 2:9), subjected Himself to death on a cross (Phil 2:8), and has therefore been exalted to the Father's right hand (Phil 2:9; Heb 1:3—now exalted over the angels once again) and "crowned with glory and honor" (Heb 2:9). This was all done as the supreme expression of the grace of God, in order that Jesus "might taste death for everyone" and bring "many sons to glory" (Heb 2:9–10).

It is a wondrous fact that Jesus Christ is still *fully human* as well as fully divine even in His exalted position with the Father, and continues to play a unique role in mediating between God and man. Paul, writing of course post-resurrection, affirms that "there *is* [not: *was*] one Mediator between God and man, the *man* Christ Jesus" (1 Tim 2:5). Similarly, Hebrews sees Christ's mediation as an ongoing rather than a completed task, using the present tense to speak of Him as the Mediator of a new and better covenant (8:6; 9:15).

The essence of Christ's atoning and mediating ministry required that He be a man (cf. Heb 2:14–17; 5:1); and Hebrews asserts repeatedly that He continues in His humanity as well as in His priestly role.[1] Psalm 110:4, quoted four times in Hebrews (5:6; 6:20; 7:17, 21) affirms that He is "a priest forever" according to the order of Melchizedek. The present tense is used repeatedly to say that we *have* (not: *had*) a great high priest (4:14, 15; 8:1; 10:21). By the agency of that priest we are now able to offer a new kind of sacrifice:

> Through him then let us continually offer up a sacrifice of praise to God, that is, the fruit of lips that acknowledge his name. Do not neglect to do good and to share what you have, for such sacrifices are pleasing to God (13:15–16).

A prominent theme of Hebrews is the continuing priestly ministry of Christ. That ministry is indeed essential to our salvation, as is clearly seen in 7:23–25:

> The former priests were many in number, because they were prevented by death from continuing in office, but he holds his priesthood permanently, because he continues forever. Consequently, he is able to save to the uttermost those who draw near to God through him, since he always lives to make intercession for them.[2]

1. "It is mainly . . . to the Author of the Epistle to the Hebrews that we turn for our understanding of the High Priesthood of Christ" (T. F. Torrance, *Royal Priesthood*, 10).

2. Other New Testament passages which speak of Christ's continuing mediating and intercessory ministry are Romans 8:34, 1 Timothy 2:5, and 1 John 2:1.

In Hebrews 10:19–22 the author makes a climactic application ("therefore," 19) of his preceding treatment of the superiority of Christ and the New Covenant: he exhorts his readers to take advantage of their privilege of access into the presence of God and encourages them to "draw near to God" (22) with boldness (19) and assurance (22). The writer says there are two reasons they can draw near: they have [ἔχοντες] "confidence to enter the holy places by the blood of Jesus, by the new and living way that he opened for us through the curtain, that is, through his flesh" (19–20)—that is, because of His *past* work; and they have "a great priest over the house of God"—that is, because of His *present* work.[3]

Because of the attacks upon the deity of Christ in the early centuries of the Church, debate and attention was naturally directed towards that aspect of Christ's nature, but at the expense of a balancing appreciation of Christ's humanity and continuing priesthood. This had far-reaching consequences for the worship of the Middle Ages, as Thomas Torrance explains:

> Arianism tended to force a heretical gloss upon the concept of the mediatorship of Christ, to which the Church became so sensitive that there was a widespread reaction against it, with the result that the human priesthood and mediation of Christ were pushed further and further into the background of worship. . . . Public worship came to be regarded, not so much as a participation through and with Christ in the

---

3. "According to Ephesians 2:18 it is through Christ that we 'have access' to the Father. Our worship is thus offered to God not only on account of what Christ has already done but also by his present mediation (*dia* with genitive, Romans 1:8; 16:27; 2 Corinthians 1:20; 1 Peter 2:5; 4:11; and the passages quoted from Ephesians and Hebrews [Heb. 2:11–18; 3:1f.; 5:1–10; 10:9f.; 6:19f.; 7:25; 10:19–22; 13:15; Eph. 2:18])" (Wainwright, *Doxology*, 62).

worship which he offers to God on behalf of all mankind, but as the regular means whereby the faithful receive divine grace and are "deified" through union with Christ in his divine nature. . . . The mediatorship and humanity of Christ fell into the background, and the poor creature was confronted immediately with the over- whelming majesty of God. . . . The Eucharist becomes, as it were, a "rival" or "substitute" for Christ as the centre of actual devotion in the worship of the Church. There arose . . . the demand for other functionaries exercising a me- diatorial ministry, to make up for the human priesthood of Christ. It is in this connection that we find the cult of the Virgin Mary as the mediatrix of the prayers of the people, and of the saints associated with her in this mediation of prayer; but above all the Church was thrown back upon itself to provide a priesthood which could stand in for Christ, and even mediate between the sinner and Christ, and therefore a priesthood which was distinct from Christ and over against him.[4]

James Torrance also speaks to the problem and de- scribes Calvin's remedy:

Fear of Arianism after Nicaea too often led the Church to play down the thought of the praying Christ, and onesidedly emphasized the role of the divine Christ as the Object of prayer. But when this happens, the tendency is for the priesthood of the Church to replace the Priesthood of Christ. The doctrine of the vicarious humanity of Christ in worship begins

4. T. F. Torrance, "The Mind of Christ in Worship," 198–99, 202–4.

to disappear. We can understand therefore why Calvin was so concerned to recover the doctrine of the sole Priesthood of Christ—to put the true Priesthood back where it belongs in the humanity of Jesus—and to reinterpret the Church in corporate terms as a royal priesthood participating in the Priesthood of Christ.[5]

We still need today to be reminded of these great truths, for we have tended to democratize (if not Pelagianize) the "priesthood of all believers" to the point where we lose sight of our need for our great High Priest to clothe us with Himself and lead us into the Father's presence.

Christ in His humanity continues to identify with us and consider us His brethren (Heb 2:11). Torrance summarizes wonderfully what He undertakes on our behalf as a result:

> Christ in His ascended *humanity* is our God-given Response, the Leader of our Worship, the Pioneer of our Faith, our Advocate and High Priest, who through the eternal Spirit presents Himself for us to the Father. In and through the mediatorial ministry of the Spirit, we worship the Father in the name of Christ.[6]

That indeed is the ministry which is so beautifully reflected in Hebrews 2:12b.

5. James B. Torrance, "Christ in Our Place," 43.
6. James B. Torrance, "The Place of Jesus Christ in Worship," 359.

The Two-Way Mediation of Christ

Thomas Torrance shows how in the Old Testament the relationship between God and His people was normally mediated by two different individuals or groups.[7]

Moses was the archetypical mediator between God and man: God communicated His message to him on the mountain, and then as God's spokesman he delivered God's Word to the people. He was the mediator *between God and man*.[8] That role was later filled by the *prophets*: we often read that "the word of the Lord came to" the prophet (Jer 1:4, etc.; Ezek 1:3, etc.; Jonah 1:1; Hag 1:1; Zech 1:1); and then it was the prophet's task to communicate to the people what the Lord had told him.

Aaron, as the first high priest, was responsible for leading the people in their response of worship back to God through the sacrificial system. He was the mediator *between man and God*. And the priesthood continued in that role throughout the Old Testament (worthily or not).

Then in the New Testament we find *both* those roles filled and fulfilled in one Person, the Mediator between God and man, Jesus Christ. A number of writers have pointed this out:

> Under the old order Moses and Aaron were prominent as apostle and high priest respectively; but in the new and eternal order the two offices of apostleship and high priesthood are combined in the one person of Jesus Christ.[9]

7. T. F. Torrance, *Royal Priesthood*, 3–5, 8–10.

8. He also served a priestly function in interceding for the people before God, especially in Exodus 32, but his primary role was as God's appointed messenger.

9. Hughes, *Hebrews*, 5.

Jesus Christ has a double ministry of representing God to man, and representing man to God. There is a God-manward movement in Jesus Christ. God (and the kingdom of God) came in Jesus Christ. But there is also a man-Godward movement (in worship, communion, prayer, loving trust, obedience, and in the self-offering of Jesus on behalf of the sins of the world). . . . Jesus Christ does not merely represent God to men in bringing God's word of forgiveness to men (dealing with men on behalf of the Father). He also represents men to God, and deals with the Father on behalf of men—as our great High Priest, our Intercessor.[10]

Jesus Christ, the same yesterday, today and forever, mediates God's blessing to us. It is through his remembered, experienced and anticipated presence, concentrated in worship, that God reaches us. Jesus embodies not only the divine initiative but also the human response, not only God's grace but also man's freedom. He prays for us and includes the motion of our attempted self-offering in his own.[11]

The initiatory "downward" movement of Christian worship begins in the Father's gracious and free revelation of the divine nature to the church through the Son, by means of the Spirit. . . . The "upward" movement of human response in worship is . . . offered to God the Father, who is the proper object of worship,

10. James B. Torrance, "The Contribution of John McLeod Campbell to Scottish Theology," 306, 309.

11. Wainwright, *Doxology*, 86.

through the Son Jesus Christ, who (being fully
divine and fully human) is the mediator of the
church's worship.[12]

The writer of Hebrews is well aware of Christ's dual
mediation. As mentioned earlier, the description of Christ
in Hebrews 3:1 as the "Apostle and High Priest of our confession" both looks back at chapters 1 and 2 in summary
of the Son's revelatory (manward) and priestly (Godward)
ministries seen there, and looks ahead to the contrast to
be drawn with both Moses and Aaron (and their respective
revelatory and priestly ministries).[13]

12. Butin, *Reformed Ecclesiology*, 25–26.

13. In fact, the structure and vocabulary of the verse emphasizes
this even further: in a chiastic arrangement, believers' status as "holy
brothers" can be seen to stem from Christ's sacrificial ministry as
priest, while they are "partakers of a heavenly calling" through Christ's
heavenly call as Apostle. "[ἀπόστολος] weist auf κλῆσις ἐπουρανίου, ἀρξιερεύς auf ἅγιοι zurück" ("[ἀπόστολος] points back to
κλῆσις ἐπουρανίου, and ἀρξιερεύς back to ἅγιοι.") (Michel, *Der
Brief an Die Hebräer*, 172). "Here the double office of Christ underlies
the description of Christians which has been given already. ἀπόστολος
gives the authority of the κλῆσις ἐπουρανίου and ἀρξιερεύς the
source of the title ἅγιοι" (Westcott, *The Epistle to the Hebrews*, 74).
"τὸν ἀπόστολον is manifestly connected with κλήσεως ἐπουρανίου
μέτοξοι, as ἀρξιερέα refers (chiastically) to ἀδελφοὶ ἅγιοι. Jesus, as
the inaugurator of the heavenly calling, is our Apostle, and as Sanctifier
our High Priest" (Delitzsch, *Hebrews*, 154).

In addition, "our confession" can be taken as an intended double
meaning with a subjective and an objective sense: connoting both our
embracing of the content of Christ's message as Apostle and our Christ-
led response of faith to that message. "Der Genitiv τῆς ὁμολογίας
ist sowohl zu ἀπόστολος als auch zu ἀρξιερεύς zu ziehen" ("The
genitive τῆς ὁμολογίας refers not only back to ἀπόστολος but
also to ἀρξιερεύς.") (Michel, *Der Brief an Die Hebräer*, 172). "Our
profession is not only to confess that Christ is God's Son but to fight
the good fight of faith and lay hold on eternal life" (Sexton, *Hebrews,
Jude, and Philemon*, 36). "Here it may be taken either for an act on our
part—the confessing Christ to be 'the Apostle and High Priest,' or, the

As we have seen, we have in 2:12 an illustration, in close juxtaposition, of the two directions of Christ's mediatorial role: 12a shows the God-to-man, revelatory trajectory of his work; 12b describes the man-to-God, responsorial trajectory.

Sanders Willson has shown how Melchizedek, the type of Christ featured so prominently in Hebrews, prefigured the bi-directional mediating ministry of Christ in Genesis 14:19–20: there we see both that *God blesses Abraham* through Melchizedek (19), and *Abraham blesses God* through Melchizedek (20).[14]

In 2 Corinthians 1:20 is another similarly beautiful crystallization of Christ's dual mediating role: God says "Yes" to all His promises "*in Him* [Christ]"; and our worship is simply our response, made "*through Him* [Christ]," to God's "Yes" to us.[15]

The Revelation-Response Pattern of Scripture

The rhythm of *revelation* and *response* is characteristic of all God's dealings with man. This ordering of these two elements is tremendously significant, for it speaks of the *initiative* which God takes, and the lengths to which He goes, to ensure a relationship with those whom He chooses. Throughout Scripture we see God's revelatory initiative with His people, with the result that all worship, obedience and service should be seen as a *response* to God's prior activity in revelation and redemption. This is true because, as Eric

---

subject matter of the faith we profess" (Pink, *Hebrews*, 156).

14. Willson, "Receiving Jesus as Priest."

15. See Man, "Yes and Amen."

Alexander has stated, "God needs to be known before He can be worshiped."[16] Nicholls expands on this idea:

> Our worship is our answer to God who has first addressed us. . . . Man worships the God who has made Himself known, and that worship is to be governed, both in fact and in form, by this revelation. We "praise His holy Name"—that is, we worship Him in His self-revelation. If God had not revealed Himself, we could not praise Him.[17]

The rhythm of revelation resulting in response, of theology leading to doxology, of God's action causing man's reaction, can be found throughout the Scriptures. Some examples:

	Revelation	Response
Life of Abraham	Covenantal promises names of God, theophanies	Builds altars, call on the name of the Lord
Exodus	Revelation of God's nature (Exod. 3, Sinai), redemption from Egypt	Song of Moses, sacrifices of redeemed people
Exodus 24:3–8	Terms of covenant	Acceptance of terms
Ten Command-ments	"I am the Lord your God, who brought you out of the land of Egypt"	"You shall have no other gods before Me"
Israel	The Law	Obedience (or not)
Neh 8	Ezra reads The Law	The people respond

16. Alexander, "Worship: The Old Testament Pattern."
17. Nicholls, *Jacob's Ladder*, 37.

	Revelation	Response
Ps 1:2	"The Law of the Lord . . .	is his delight."
Ps 48:10	As is Your Name, O God . . ,"	so is Your praise to the ends of the earth." (NASB)
Ps 96:4	"Great is the Lord . . .	and greatly to be praised."
Ps 100	"The Lord is God" (3) "The Lord is good" (5)	"shout" "serve" "come" (1–2) "enter" "praise" "give thanks" (4)
Ps 150:2	. . . according to His excellent greatness."	"Praise Him . . .
Isa 6:1–5	"I saw the Lord"	"Woe is me!"
Luke 2:10	"I bring you good news of . . .	a great joy which will be for all the people"
Jesus	Life (revealed the Father)	Death (propitiatory sacrifice)
Rom 1:20–21	God's attributes, power, nature clearly seen	"they did not honor Him as God or give thanks"
2 Cor. 1:20	God says yes to us *in* Christ	We reply "Amen" *through* Christ
Heb 2:12	"I will proclaim Your Name to My brethren . . .	and in the midst of the congregation I will sing Your praise"
Heb 3:1	Apostle	High Priest

Calvin speaks also to this natural progression: "The proclamation of God's praises is always promoted by the teaching of the gospel; for as soon as God becomes known

to us, His infinite praises resound in our hearts and ears."[18]
To which Butin adds:

> The initiatory "downward" movement of
> Christian worship begins in the Father's gracious
> and free revelation of the divine nature to the
> church through the Son, by means of the Spirit.
> In more concrete terms, this takes place in the
> proclamation of the Word according to scripture,
> by the empowerment and illumination of the
> Spirit. . . . The "upward" movement of human
> response in worship—focused around prayer
> and the celebration of the sacraments . . . —is
> also fundamentally motivated by God. Human
> response—"the sacrifice of praise and thanksgiv-
> ing"—arises from the faith that has its source in
> the indwelling Holy Spirit. In that Spirit, prayer,
> devotion, and obedience are offered to God the
> Father, who is the proper object of worship,
> through the Son Jesus Christ, who (being fully
> divine and fully human) is the mediator of the
> church's worship.[19]

So too should our worship services be a true dialogue,
with alternating revelation and response: hearing from
God (through His Word, read and sung and prayed and
preached)[20] and replying to Him (with our songs and prayers
and confession and the Lord's Supper).[21] Historically, this
pattern underlies both Old Testament worship (in covenant
establishment and renewal[22]) and Christian worship (in the

18. Calvin, *Hebrews and the First and Second Epistles of St. Peter*, 27.

19. Butin, *Reformed Ecclesiology*, 102.

20. Most evangelical services need more Scripture so that the
sermon is not the only (belated) element of revelation (see chapter 5,
section 4 below).

21. See Furr and Price, *The Dialogue of Worship*.

22. Hilber, "Theology of Worship in Exodus 24," 177–89.

Word-Table structure found in most historical liturgies[23]). It is also reflected in the Anglican Christmastime service of "*Lessons* [revelation] *and Carols* [response]."

The pattern of revelation and response is clearly portrayed in the two halves, respectively, of Hebrews 2:12; and most importantly (and blessedly), the Person of the living Christ is seen as the agent and mediator of *both* of those activities.

---

23. Webber, *Worship Old and New*, 49–79.

5

Towards a Christology
of Worship

HEBREWS 2:12 may well serve as a touchstone or entry
point for a more developed and deeper understanding of Christ's central role in the worship of the Church.
The following themes are consonant with and enriched by
what we have looked at in our study of the meaning and
significance of Hebrews 2:12.

*1. The living Christ is present in our midst when we gather
for worship.*

Far from being a nostalgic remembrance of One who
once walked among us, Christian worship should be a celebra-
tion of a *living* and *active* Savior who promised to "never leave
you or forsake you" (Heb 13:5) and to be "with you always,
to the end of the age" (Matt 28:20). He is always among us as
the Mediator, the "Jacob's Ladder" between God and man and
between man and God. Our great High Priest is present not
only in the heavenly tabernacle (Heb 8:2), leading us into the
very presence of the Holy One; but is also in His deity (and,
through the Holy Spirit, even in His humanity) present in every gathering of His brethren, guiding us into a knowledge and
experience of being seated with Him "in the heavenly places"
(Eph 1:3; 2:6) even while here on earth.

A corollary corrective flowing out of this truth is that
we do not have to invite God to join us when we gather, or
hope that He will "show up" (as the common parlance puts
it) if we can only worship right. He never left! Rather we
are the invited, and we need to "show up" and key into the
true reality of Christ's welcoming presence. He did not just
open or point out the way for us, but actively leads us into
the Father's presence.[1]

As Karen Burton Mains has movingly put it:

> We need to remind ourselves, over and over,
> that the focus of Sunday worship must be upon
> the living Christ among us. In truth, if Christ
> were bodily present and we could see Him
> with more than our soul's eyes, all our worship
> would become intentional. If Christ stood on
> our platforms, we would bend our knees with-
> out asking. If He stretched out His hands and
> we saw the wounds, our hearts would break;
> we would confess our sins and weep over our
> shortcomings. If we could hear His voice lead-
> ing the hymns, we too would sing heartily;
> the words would take on meaning. The Bible
> reading would be lively; meaning would pierce
> to the marrow of our souls. If Christ walked
> our aisles, we would hasten to make amends
> with that brother or sister to whom we have
> not spoken. We would volunteer for service,
> the choir loft would be crowded. If we knew
> Christ would attend our church Sunday after
> Sunday, the front pews would fill fastest, believ-
> ers would arrive early, offering plates would be
> laden with sacrificial but gladsome gifts, prayers
> would concentrate our attention. Yet, the star-

---

1. "Our worship is not just . . . because of the works and merits
of Christ, but . . . through the Person of Christ Himself" (James B.
Torrance, "Christ in Our Place," 43).

tling truth is that Christ *is* present, through His Holy Spirit, in our churches; it is we who must develop eyes to see and ears to hear Him.[2]

2. Only in and through Christ can we enter into God's presence in worship.

Nicholls rightly insists, "Without the work of Christ, bringing God down to men, and gathering men in Himself before God, there can be no worship at all, and indeed no Church."[3] Calvin approvingly quoted Ambrose along these same lines: "'He,' says Ambrose, 'is our mouth by which we speak to the Father; our eye by which we see the Father; our right hand by which we offer ourselves to the Father. Save by his intercession neither we nor any saints have any intercourse with God.' (Ambros. Lib. de Isaac et Anima)."[4]

Christ is the essence, enabler, empowerer, channel, guide, activator, offerer[5] and mediator of all true worship. Worship is only possible in Him and through Him, by His grace and in His name. He is the "one Mediator between God and men, the man Christ Jesus" (1 Tim 2:5). He is the Ladder between heaven and earth, the "bridge across the great divide." He is the only Way,[6] but He is an all-sufficient

2. Mains, "Introduction," 5.

3. Nicholls, *Jacob's Ladder*, 36.

4. Calvin, *Institutes*, III.20.21.

5. "That is what it means to pray and worship in the name of Jesus Christ 'Mediator, High Priest and Advocate'; He is *the* Offerer of all our worship to God" (T. F. Torrance, "The Mind of Christ in Worship," 184).

6. "It is the Redeemer leading the praises of His redeemed. Strangers to God may go through all the outward forms of mere 'religion,' but they never *praise* God. It is only upon resurrection ground that worship is possible" (Pink, *An Exposition of Hebrews*, 123).

Way. How Pelagianism and its offshoots do violence to that utter sufficiency![7]

As Thomas and James Torrance both make clear, our worship is *His* worship, our position before the Father is *His* position, our access[8] to the Father is *His* access:

> He has once and for all offered to God our obedience, our response, our witness, our amen. He became our brother man and he offered on our behalf a human obedience, a human response, a human witness and a human amen, so that in Him our human answer to God in life, worship, and prayer is already completed. He is in the fullest sense our ὁμολογία. It can only be ours, therefore, if it involves the setting aside (ἀθέτησις) of the obedience, response, witness, amen, and even the worship and prayer which we offer on our own. The radical significance of Christ's substitutionary Priesthood does not lie in the fact that His perfect Self-offering perfects and completes our imperfect offerings, but that these are displaced by His completed Self-offering. We can only offer what has already been offered on our behalf, and offer it by the only mode appropriate to such a substitutionary offering, by prayer, thanksgiving and praise.[9]

---

7. "Such an unique Intermediary evangelical faith recognizes in her beloved Lord. Alas that Rome, with her understudy, Anglo-Catholicism, robs Him of the homage which it pays to a Church that 'succeeds Him on earth in the exercise of His priestly office' (W. P. Patterson)" (Simpson, "The Vocabulary of the Epistle to the Hebrews," 188).

8. "For *through him* we both have access in one Spirit to the Father" (Eph 2:18).

9. T. F. Torrance, *Royal Priesthood*, 14.

> Our worship of God takes place . . . through
> Jesus himself as a worshipper of God, and wor-
> shipper in our place. Unless that is kept central,
> the liturgical language "through Jesus Christ
> our Lord" or even "through Jesus Christ our
> Mediator and High Priest" can easily degenerate
> into mere formulae to which we attach our own
> self-erected worship without the actual media-
> tion of Christ in his vicarious humanity.[10]

> His Humanity is our humanity (so graciously
> assumed), His Death our death (which we shew
> forth), His Life our life (till He come), His Self-
> Offering our offering, His Communion with
> the Father our communion, into which He lifts
> us by His Spirit.[11]

As Liesch summarizes the view of James Torrance, "The
real agent in worship, in a New Testament understanding,
is Jesus Christ, who leads us in our praises and prayers, 'the
one true minister of the sanctuary.'"[12] The essence of New
Testament worship is thus found in the Person of Jesus Christ,
living and active in His Church, as Poythress expresses:

> The essence of the regulative principle is that
> our worship must be in Christ: it is conformity
> in thought, word, and deed, heart, soul, mind,
> and strength, corporately and individually, to
> the sovereign, glorious, exalted ministry of
> Christ, as prophet, priest, and king, at the right
> hand of God.[13]

10. T. F. Torrance, "The Mind of Christ in Worship," 211.

11. James B. Torrance, "The Place of Jesus Christ in Worship,"
360.

12. Liesch, *The New Worship*, 141.

13. Poythress, "Ezra 3," 232.

Sinclair Ferguson concurs:

> All worship flows from Christ's leadership and
> through Christ's mediation. . . . He is not only
> the Mediator of our reconciliation; He is the
> Mediator of our adoration in worship. Indeed,
> . . . [we read] in Hebrews 8:2 that in that
> heavenly sanctuary we have Jesus Christ as *lei-
> tourgos*, as our worship leader. . . . That's why
> I said these amazing creatures [in Revelation
> 4—5] are really deputy worship leaders:
> Jesus Christ is the worship leader of heaven's
> glory—ascended in our humanity, bringing all
> of us by His grace before the throne of His
> Father and saying (as you remember, Hebrews
> 2[:13] cites the words of Isaiah and puts them
> into the lips of our Lord Jesus), "Father, here I
> am, and the children You have given Me." He
> gathers us into [God's] presence, leads us in
> our praises.[14]

3. *Our worship is pleasing and acceptable to God not
   because of its own excellence, but because of (and only
   because of) the excellence of His Son.*

Jungmann identifies the true source of worship's power:

> The Church's prayers of praise to God gain
> meaning and value only because Christ as high
> priest stands at her head and joins in them.
> Through Him, God is constantly paid the
> highest honor, even without our help, since his
> divine glorified humanity is the finest flower of
> creation, the supreme revelation of God.[15]

14. Sinclair Ferguson, "The Church's Worship."
15. Jungmann, *The Place of Christ*, 137.

God accepts and delights in our worship, not because of our efforts or our artistry or even our spirituality, but because of the Son's continual offering of worship in our place and on our behalf. He gathers up our imperfect expressions of worship into His own perfect one. It is not the excellence of our worship (quality, quantity or form) which makes it acceptable and pleasing unto God, but the excellence of His Son, with Whom He is eternally well-pleased (Matt 3:17; 17:5; 2 Pet 1:17). As Glodo aptly puts it:

> The beauty of our worship, just as our righteousness before God, is not found in ourselves but in Jesus. The voice of Jesus singing with us perfects our worship as it reaches the throne of God.[16]

Thomas Torrance also has spoken to this issue effectively in various writings:

> Through, with and in Christ our worship and prayer are grounded in him in such a way that we may come before God the Father without playing a role or without having to look over our shoulder at what we are doing, out of anxiety lest it be wrong or unworthy, or simply out of a desire to be (or appear to be) pious, or out of a determination to use worship and prayer as a means of spiritual discipline. Who does indeed come before God without ulterior motives of some kind corrupting his intention? But to worship and pray through, with and in Christ is to worship God for God's sake, with the perfection of true worship which Christ is, and not in some secret way for our own sake. Through, with and in Christ we turn away in penitential self-denial from our own acts of worship and prayer in order to rest in the worship and prayer

16. Glodo, "Singing with the Savior."

which our Saviour has already offered and continues to offer to the Father on our behalf.[17]

The Church on earth lives and acts only as it is directed by its heavenly Lord, and only in such a way that his Ministry is reflected in the midst of its ministry and worship. Therefore from first to last the worship and ministry of the Church on earth must be governed by the fact that Christ substitutes himself in our place, and that our humanity with its own acts of worship, is displaced by his, so that we appear before God not in our own name, not in our own significance, not in virtue of our own acts of confession, contrition, worship, and thanksgiving, but solely in the name of Christ and solely in virtue of what he has done in our name and on our behalf, and in our stead. Justification by Christ alone means that from first to last in the worship of God and in the ministry of the Gospel Christ himself is central, and that we draw near in worship and service only through letting him take our place. He only is Priest. He only represents humanity. He only has an offering with which to appear before God and with which God is well-pleased. He only presents our prayers before God, and he only is our praise and thanksgiving and worship as we appear before the face of the Father.[18]

We do not come before God, then, worshipping him and praying to him in our own name, or in our own significance, but in the name and significance of Jesus Christ alone, for worship

17. T. F. Torrance, "The Mind of Christ in Worship," 211–12.
18. T. F. Torrance, *Theology in Reconstruction*, 167.

and prayer are not ways in which we express ourselves but ways in which we hold up before the Father his beloved Son, take refuge in his atoning sacrifice, and make that our only plea.

> *"Nothing in my hands I bring;*
> *Simply to thy Cross I cling."*[19]

The only thing that ultimately matters is engaging with the Son through the Holy Spirit in our worship, and then resting in the confidence and assurance with which we are invited to "draw near to God" in and through Him (Heb 10:19–22).

This truth means that the little country church with an out-of-tune piano and screechy singers can be just as pleasing to God (and perhaps more so) than the huge suburban mega-church with a full symphony orchestra or a professional-caliber praise band. As C.S. Lewis reminded us, we are not going to be able to impress God no matter what musical forces we muster:

> We must beware of the naïve idea that our music can "please" God as it would please a cultivated human hearer. That is like thinking, under the old Law, that He really needed the blood of bulls and goats. To which an answer came, "mine are the cattle upon a thousand hills", and "if I am hungry, I will not tell *thee*." If God (in that sense) wanted music, He would not tell *us*. For all our offerings, whether of music or martyrdom, are like the intrinsically worthless present of a child, which a father values indeed, but values only for the intention.[20]

---

19. T. F. Torrance, *The Mediation of Christ*, 97–98.
20. Lewis, "On Church Music," 98–99.

To that we would only hasten to add the perspective of *Christ's* offering, which is of intrinsic and infinite value to the Father. And so the writer of Hebrews near the end of his epistle makes a grand application which draws up into it so much of what has gone before when he urges us: "Through *him* [Christ] then let us continually offer up a sacrifice of praise to God" (Heb 13:15).

Robert Webber sums up well the freedom which this truth gives us:

> Who can love God with his heart, mind, and soul?
> Who can achieve perfect union with God?
> Who can worship God with a pure and unstained heart?
> Not me! . . .
> Not you. Not Billy Graham. . . .
> Not anybody I know or you know.
> Only Jesus can. And he does for me and for you what
>   neither of us can do for ourselves.

> This is the message that is missing in the literature of contemporary worship. It is too much about what I ought to do and too little about what God has done for me. God has done for me what I cannot do for myself. He did it in Jesus Christ. Therefore my worship is offered in a broken vessel that is in the process of being healed, but is not yet capable of fullness of joy, endless intense passion, absolute exaltation, and celebration. But Jesus, who shares in my humanity yet without sin, is not only my Savior—he is also my complete and eternal worship, doing for me, in my place, what I cannot do. . . .

> He is eternally interceding to the Father on our behalf. And for this reason, our worship is always in and through Christ. . . .

> Thanks for Jesus Christ, who is my worship. We are free! And in gratitude, we offer our

stumbling worship in the name of Jesus with thanksgiving.[21]

Ben Patterson has provided a beautiful illustration of this truth:

> Ignace Jan Paderewski was, at one time, both the prime minister of Poland and a virtuoso pianist. A story is told about a mother who brought her young son to hear him perform. The boy was just beginning to learn the piano and she wanted him to hear a master, so she bought tickets for two front-row seats in the concert hall. They sat down a few minutes before the concert was to begin.
>
> In the excitement of the event, the mother was looking around the large hall, mesmerized by the glitter and festivity. She didn't notice when her son climbed up on the stage, walked over to the piano and sat down on the bench. Suddenly she, and everyone else in the auditorium, heard the tune "Chopsticks" coming from the piano on the stage. To her embarrassment and horror, she turned to discover that her son was committing this sacrilege upon the master's piano.
>
> Before she could get up on the stage and stop the boy, the master himself walked out from behind the curtains. Paderewski smiled at the distraught mother and waved her back to her seat. He then stood behind the boy, reached around him with both hands and began to play a lovely obbligato to his "Chopsticks." They were coworkers but not co-equals.

---

21. Webber, "A Blended Worship Response," 130.

> We become coworkers with God only when
> he reaches around the feeble work of our hands
> with his hands and sanctifies it.[22]

Similarly, Cocksworth insists it is still "our worship," but not only *our* worship:

> I am not much of a singer. I find it difficult to
> stay in tune. But when I stand next to someone
> with a fine voice I find it much easier. The voice
> I hear in my ear helps to keep my voice on line
> and I like to think of my voice merging with
> that voice so that the faltering poverty of mine
> is purified and beautified by the richness of the
> other. This is a crude and very inadequate re-
> flection of what happens when we worship. The
> integrity of the worship which comes from our
> lips and our hearts is retained—it remains our
> worship—but it is retuned by the greater in-
> tegrity of the worship of Christ. The Spirit lifts
> our prayer and praise into the sphere of Christ's
> worship to be purified and perfected by his
> prayer and praise and then presented by Christ
> to the Father in its new and redeemed form.
> Our worship is *with* Christ our brother, *in*
> Christ our priest but always *through* Christ our
> sacrifice, whose death once for us is the means
> of our cleansing, renewing and perfecting.[23]

4. *The Word of God, by which Christ proclaims His Father's name to His brethren, deserves priority and centrality in our worship.*

In our study in Hebrews 2:12 we have seen that it is the ministry of the glorified Christ in the midst of His people to mediate the revelation of God's glorious name

22. Patterson, *Serving God*, 159–60.
23. Cocksworth, *Holy, Holy, Holy*, 161–62.

and nature. Christ wants to speak to us on behalf of God, through His Word and through His spokesmen and in the power of the Holy Spirit. We need to listen! If worship is to be dialogue, there must be an interplay between God's speaking to us and our response back to him—we must not do all of the talking!

Many evangelical churches sadly neglect the reading of Scripture in worship services. Though we may pride ourselves on being "people of the Book," the fact is that there are countless liberal churches where there is far more Scripture heard (especially in the standard liturgies) than in many if not most free churches in the evangelical tradition!

And God deserves to have the first word. A common practice is to enter right into songs of praise without even a call to worship (which many consider old-fashioned or, worse yet, "liturgical"). Yet the biblical paradigm for worship and indeed for all of God's dealing with mankind, that of revelation and response, logically demands hearing first from God so that we have something to legitimately respond to with our worship.[24] Only then is our worship an appropriate response to His self-revelation.

There was a similar problem in Old Testament Israel. We should consider ourselves warned as Thomas Torrance describes

> the attempt . . . to make the sacrificial priest-
> hood stand by itself, independently of the me-
> diation of the Word. That is the story of Israel
> all through the centuries. . . . The tendency to
> make the sacrificial priesthood independent
> of the prophetic Word for God represents

24. What in effect is happening in such churches is that there is an unconscious reliance on a reservoir of knowledge of God on the part of the people, which they can draw upon as they begin with praise. But how much better to hear directly from God through His Word, and immediately respond to what we have heard!

the temptation to escape from direct meeting or encounter with the living God. . . . [In a footnote he adds here: "Essentially the same temptations later assailed the Christian Church in the Mediterranean countries."] That was certainly the great sin of Israel. She sought to make the Temple and its liturgy independent of God's Word . . . so that it became a liturgy of oblation as action upon God, as manipulation of God's will.[25]

James White has identified the potential of damaging spiritual effects from the negligence of Bible reading in our worship:

If the bulletin makes it clear that scripture is an important part of Christian worship, then we can be sure people will get the message that the Bible is crucial in shaping their lives as Christians. But, when the role of scripture in worship is negligible, when scripture is used only to launch a sermon, what is communicated is that the Bible is marginal in Christian life, too. The use we make or fail to make of scripture in our worship says far more about Christian discipleship than we may realize.[26]

We need to allow Christ the fullness of His ministry in speaking to His people about His Father through the Word.

5. *The corporate praise of God's people is an integral and crucial part of the gathering of the church.*

The sermon was king in most twentieth-century evangelical churches. Pastors and many others tended to regard the singing and other parts of the service as mere

25. T. F. Torrance, *Royal Priesthood*, 5.
26. White, "Making Our Worship More Biblical," 88.

preliminaries to the homiletical "main event." Actually this tendency arose from at least two sources.

One, as White points out, was nineteenth-century revivalism in the United States and its formula, used successfully in camp meetings and other evangelistic gatherings, where the speaker was indeed the main attraction and all that went before was consciously intended to "warm up" the audience. This approach was carried over (both consciously and unconsciously in different places, it would seem) more or less intact into the worship services in what White calls the "Frontier" tradition of American Protestantism—where it is still alive and well in many churches![27]

The other strain comes from a quite different direction, namely the Reformed tradition. Here the exposition of the Scriptures has received due emphasis and honor, but sometimes to the extent that "we neglect the rest of the worship service (sometimes demeaningly called the preliminaries), and rest content, as the reformers never were, with infrequent communion."[28] Hageman points out that Zwingli banned all music whatsoever from worship, and that were it not for Calvin instituting Psalm-singing, Reformed churches might still have no music! Hageman offers a reasonable rationale: "What is the proper place of music in a service of Reformed worship? To provide a suitable opportunity for the congregation to respond to the Word of God."[29]

Quite simply put, the biblical paradigm of revelation and response is not completed unless there is a response on the part of those who have heard the revelation. As John Stott puts it:

> There should be no theology without doxology. There is something fundamentally flawed

27. White, "The Missing Jewel of the Evangelical Church," 103–8.
28. Stephen Farris, "Reformed Identity and Reformed Worship," 71.
29. Hageman, "Can Church Music Be Reformed?" 19–20, 23–24.

about a purely academic interest in God. God
is not an appropriate object for cool, critical,
detached, scientific observation and evaluation.
No, the true knowledge of God will always lead
us to worship, as it did Paul. Our place is on our
faces before him in adoration.[30]

God created us and revealed Himself to us and redeemed us so that we might return to Him the worship for
which we were intended, as Tozer wrote:

The purpose of God sending His Son to die and
rise and live and be at the right hand of God the
Father was that He might restore to us the missing jewel, the jewel of worship; that we might
come back and learn to do again that which we
were created to do in the first place—worship
the Lord in the beauty of holiness, to spend
our time in awesome wonder and adoration of
God, feeling and expressing it, and letting it get
into our labors and doing nothing except as an
act of worship to Almighty God through His
Son Jesus Christ.[31]

We do not come to church in order to simply hear a
sermon; rather we come to dialogue with God, to learn of
Him and be changed by Him, to respond with heart and lips
and lives of worship and obedience and service. This fact was
not lost on past generations, as Wainwright points out:

The ascription of praise with which a Chrysostom,
an Augustine, or a Calvin ended their sermons
was no mere formality: It indicated the intention
of the sermon itself and its aim of bringing oth-

30. Stott, *Romans*, 312.
31. Tozer, *Worship: The Missing Jewel*, 8.

ers also to the praise of God on account of what
had been proclaimed in Scripture and sermon.[32]

If all of life is to be worship (Rom 12:1) in response
to all that God has done for us in Christ ("Therefore . . . by
the mercies of God"), then that response certainly belongs
in the public gatherings of the church, where the nature and
promises and gospel of God are proclaimed.

The case may be made more strongly yet: To the notion
that the first part of the worship service is inconsequential,[33]
one may reply (on the basis of this study) that Jesus Himself
begs to differ! *He* understands the balance of revelation and
response, the need for dialogue and for completing the
circuit which He himself begins as He mediates to us the
truth of God (2:12a). He thinks that the response of praise
is so important that He is right in the middle of it, initiat-
ing it and leading it! To be sure, the revelation part of the
equation takes precedence—but not so as to denigrate the
response. Jesus Christ Himself indwells and empowers and
mediates and leads that response, demonstrating its dignity
and importance. Ferguson rightly points out: "That's why
the dichotomy between worship and preaching is so unbib-
lical—because the Jesus who leads us in our praises is the
same one whose voice is heard by His sheep in the ministry
of the Word."[34]

This truth also wonderfully resolves the debate about
whether worship consists of God giving to us, or us giving

32. Wainwright, "The Praise of God in the Theological Reflection
of the Church," 38.

33. "We so stress that God comes to us as God to address
us through his Word in preaching that we short-circuit the real
humanity of Christ, the role of the continuing priesthood of Christ in
representing us to God, and have a one-sided view of the work of the
Spirit" (James B. Torrance, *Worship, Community and the Triune God
of Grace*, 88–89).

34. Sinclair Ferguson, "The Church's Worship."

to God. Which is true? *Both*, in Christ who is at the center of both activities.

> 6. *No matter how they may differ in the externals, all true expressions of worship share in common that they are led and mediated by Christ in the power of the Holy Spirit.*

"No matter what the externals . . . of the new worship of the New Covenant people may be, it has . . . as its center . . . the presence of the crucified, risen, reigning and ministering Lord Jesus Christ."[35]

In spite of a huge diversity in worship styles and practices, in music and dress and architecture and forms and customs, from church to church, culture to culture, continent to continent, century to century throughout the history of the Church—the fact remains that there is a constant thread wherever true worship is taking place: it is the role of the living Christ in the midst of His people, leading their worship. James Torrance stresses that "there is only one way to come to the Father, namely through Christ in the communion of saints, whatever outward form our worship may take."[36] And Ferguson concurs when he speaks of "that which is really central in our worship—namely the Lord Jesus Himself."[37]

God has obviously been pleased to accept a wide array of differing expressions of praise to His great name—but only if those praises are offered up through and in the name of His dear Son. As Kidd has stirringly described this situation (on the basis of Hebrews 2:12 and the context of its quotation from Psalm 22):

---

35. Ferguson, "True Spirituality, True Worship."
36. James B. Torrance, "The Doctrine of the Trinity," 6.
37. Ferguson, "True Spirituality, True Worship."

Every group brings its own voice, but no group brings the official voice. One Voice sings above them all, and this Voice sings in all their voices, excluding none. His singular voice is distributed among a plurality of people. Just because there are so many dimensions to His own being, the multiplicity of their voices amplifies His song. . . .

Jesus . . . sings folk idioms from "all the families of the earth" [Ps 22:27], purging the idolatrous and focusing the yearning for redemption that shows up wherever the *imago Dei* bears the kiss of common grace. From the very start, Jesus' ministry displayed an outwardboundness that was scandalous to His own kin. He had the nations in view from start to finish—that is who He is: God's heart for all the families of the earth.

What I believe we have seen in twenty centuries of church music is Christ calling forth His song from every culture His gospel has touched. Even when believers attempt distinctly "Christian" music, their music invariably bears the marks of their social world, and indeed would be incomprehensible without those marks. . . . Jesus sings God's covenantal faithfulness and the width of His mercy in as many musical dialects as there are peoples who embrace Him.[38]

Christ is the constant, always in the midst of His people and in their place, taking up their varied expressions of worship and incorporating them into His perfect offering of worship to the Father. He is singing the Father's praise in many languages and styles!

And so we have an argument which is simultaneously an argument for a monolithic view of the true nature of

38. Kidd, "Bach, Bubba, and the Blues Brothers."

worship *and* for a wide diversity of forms of expression in worship! As Thomas Torrance explains it:

> However much, therefore, worship and prayer may vary in linguistic and behavioural forms, as they inevitably and rightly do when they are expressed in the habits of different societies, peoples, cultures and ages, they nevertheless have embedded in them an invariant element which derives from the normative pattern of the incarnate love of God in Jesus Christ. In so far as worship and prayer are through, with and in Christ, they are not primarily forms of man's self-expression or self-fulfilment or self-transcendence in this or that human situation or cultural context, but primarily forms of Christ's vicarious worship and prayer offered on behalf of all mankind in all ages. However, precisely because our worship and prayer are finally shaped and structured by the invariant pattern of Christ's mediatorial office, they are also open to change in variant human situations and societies, cultures, languages and ages, even with respect to differing aesthetic tastes and popular appeal, if only because these variant forms of worship and prayer are relativised by the invariant form of worship and prayer in Christ which they are intended to serve. Hence when worship and prayer are objectively grounded in Christ in this way, we are free to use and adapt transient forms of language and culture in our worship of God, without being imprisoned in time-conditioned patterns, or swept along by constantly changing fashions, and without letting worship and prayer dissolve

away into merely cultural and secular forms of man's self-expression and self-fulfilment.[39]

To which Reggie Kidd adds:

> When seen in the light of the person of Jesus, the church's Lead Worshiper, our squabbles over how to do it right, which group's aesthetic will be honored, and which group's dishonored take on their true measure: they are pathetically small-minded.
>
> While we try to pare His song down to a manageable repertoire, He is expanding it. While we are doing market research to decide whom we want to reach and, therefore, to whose aesthetic tastes we want to pander, the Singing Savior is distributing His magnificent voice across an increasingly wide spectrum of musical idioms. While we are dividing congregations along age lines, He is blending the songs of generations and nations and families and tribes and tongues to make sweet harmony, precisely through the differences, to the Father.
>
> The day has come for us to mute our provincial songs, and start listening for His voice, for it is "like the sound of many waters" (Revelation 1:15), as rich and complex as the constitution of His people.
>
> Jesus' voice is what counts, not ours. And His is the voice of the Jew and the Gentile, the poor and the rich, those who have already had their say and those who have not yet even come into being. There is a unity and diversity in the voices of His assembly which we may not be able to hold together on our own, but which

---

39. T. F. Torrance, "The Mind of Christ in Worship," 213.

the Risen Christ, because He is literally and vibrantly present among us, can.[40]

> Jesus' voice is what counts, not ours; and his voice in "the great assembly" is as rich and complex as the constitution of his people. There is a unity and diversity in the voices of his assembly which we would not be able to hold together on our own. . . . If it pleases Jesus to distribute his voice among a wide range of singers and musical dialects, it would profit us to accommodate our preferences and principles to his.[41]

7. *When we preach or lead worship, we do so representing Christ* whose ministry it is. *He is the preacher; He is the worship leader.*

Boundless dignity is given to the roles of both preacher (and teacher of the Word in any context, for that matter) and worship leader, when it is considered that in both one is representing Jesus Christ, who is the true Agent and Mediator of those ministries.[42] And this truth also calls for great humility as we exercise those ministries. It is not *my* ministry of teaching, *my* preaching ministry, *my* worship ministry—it is Christ's, and I am merely standing in for Him, so to speak, as His channel and mouthpiece, in the power of the Holy Spirit.

This truth has been more commonly recognized on the preaching side of the equation:

> The preacher's place in the Church is sacramental. . . . He mediates the word to the Church from faith to faith, from his faith to theirs, from

40. Kidd, "Bach, Bubba, and the Blues Brothers."

41. Kidd, *With One Voice,* 145–46.

42. As Jesus told the seventy, "The one who listens to you listens to Me" (Luke 10:16).

one stage of their common faith to another. . . .
He is a living element in Christ's hands (broken,
if need be) for the distribution and increment
of Grace.[43]

A true sermon is an act of God, and not a
mere performance by man. In real preaching
the speaker is the servant of the word and God
speaks and works by the word through his
servant's lips.[44]

The essence of the continuing ministry of the
Church, as in the book of Acts, is "the abid-
ing activity of Christ with and through his
messengers."[45]

But it is just as true in the ministry of leading corporate
praise; Calvin (obviously a strong advocate of preaching!)
reminds us that "Christ heeds our praise, and is the chief
Conductor of our hymns."[46] Even the common title of "worship leader" seems a misnomer when one realizes that it is
Christ Himself who is the leader of His brethren's worship.

Spurgeon understood the balance perfectly and expressed it incisively:

In the great universal church Jesus is the One
authoritative teacher, and all others, so far as
they are worthy to be called teachers, are nothing but echoes of his voice. Jesus, in this second
sentence [Ps 22:22b/Heb 2:12b], reveals his
object in declaring the divine name, it is that

43. Whale, *What Is a Living Church?* 64 n.1.

44. Packer and Coates, *Beyond the Battle for the Bible*, 101.

45. Bruce, *What the Bible Teaches About What Jesus Did*, 49.

46. Calvin, *Hebrews and the First and Second Epistles of St. Peter*,
27.

God may be praised; the church continually magnifies Jehovah for manifesting himself in the person of Jesus, and Jesus himself leads the song, and is both precentor and preacher in his church.[47]

8. *Because Christ leads us in our worship, we can enter boldly and confidently into God's presence.*

As seen earlier, the writer of Hebrews summarizes in 10:19–22 that we can and should "draw near to God" (22), with boldness and assurance, because of both the past (19–20) *and* the present (21) work of Christ.

Saphir, reflecting on this great truth, writes:

> Christians, if Jesus is our brother; if Jesus and we are both of one; if Jesus says, "I will sing thy praise in the midst of the congregation;" if He is the leader of our prayers and praises before the throne of God, then we may approach the Father without fear and without doubt! Christ's peace is our peace, and our worship is the worship of perfect acceptance, of perfect trust and love in union with the Head of the Church. . . . Where is doubt now? For is Jesus in doubt of His acceptance with the Father? . . . Now He presents the Father our sacrifice of thanksgiving, our adoration, our petitions, and the Father hears the voice of Jesus in the voice of the church.[48]

9. *By His grace God has provided in Christ the worship He requires of us.*

Augustine proclaimed his utter dependence upon the grace of God:

47. Spurgeon, *Treasury of David*, on Psalm 22:22.
48. Saphir, *The Great High Priest*, 147.

> What is Thy will, O most loving Father, except
> that I should love Thee? Behold, Thou comman-
> dest that I should love Thee with all my heart
> and soul, with all my mind and strength. . . .
> But grant Thou me what Thou commandest,
> and command what Thou wilt.[49]

The grace of God means *God providing for us what He requires of us.* This is an amazing truth, and one which infinitely distinguishes Christianity from all other faiths.

God's grace is provided to us for *salvation*: providing in Christ the righteousness which heaven requires but of which we are by nature incapable. God's grace is sufficient for our *sanctification*: providing in Christ, and through the Holy Spirit, growth into the practical holiness which God demands of us 1 Pet 1:15–16.[50] *And* God's grace is made available for our *worship* as well: providing in Christ the perfect worship which He expects and deserves, but to which on our own we cannot attain. Glodo points this out:

> The beauty of our worship, just as our righ-
> teousness before God, is not found in our-
> selves but in Jesus. The voice of Jesus singing
> with us perfects our worship as it reaches the
> throne of God. While Christ's righteousness is
> the answer to our doubt about God accepting
> us, Christ's worship is the answer to our doubt
> about God being pleased with our worship. In
> this we see that our life with God is by grace
> from beginning to end.[51]

49. Augustine, *Confessions*, X.31.

50. That sanctification is a work of God and His grace is amply attested to by the New Testament: Rom 8:26; Gal 3:3; Phil 2:12–13; 1Thess 5:23; Titus 2:11–12; Heb 13:20–21. 1 Peter 4:11 explains that God works in this way "in order that in everything God may be glorified through Jesus Christ."

51. Glodo, "Singing with the Savior."

By God's grace we *can* come to God in worship because of Christ's past atoning work; and by His grace He
also enables and empowers our worship by means of Christ's
continuing mediating ministry. James Torrance has spoken
powerfully of God's gracious provision for our worship in a
number of places:

> [Such is] the Gospel of grace, that our Father
> in the gift of his Son and the gift of the Spirit,
> gives us what he demands—the worship of our
> hearts and minds—lifting us up out of ourselves
> to participate in the very life of the Godhead.[52]

> God does not throw back upon ourselves to make
> our response to the Word in our own strength.
> But graciously he helps our infirmities by giving
> us Jesus Christ and the Holy Spirit to make the
> appropriate response for us and in us.[53]

52. James B. Torrance, "The Doctrine of the Trinity," 5.

53. James B. Torrance, *Worship, Community and the Triune God
of Grace*, 89. Elsewhere he adds: "Such is the wonderful love of God,
that He has come to us in Jesus Christ, and in Jesus assumed our life
(the life of all men), underwritten our responsibilities, offered for us
a life of worship and obedience and prayer to the Father, taken to
Himself our body of death, vicariously submitted for us to the verdict
of 'guilty,' died our death and risen again in our humanity, so that by
the grace of God, His life is our life, His death is our death, His victory
our victory, His resurrection our resurrection, His righteousness our
righteousness and His eternal prayers and self-offerings to the Father
our prayers and offering in the presence of the Father. So we are
accepted in the Beloved, and discover our status as sons.

"*By grace* God gives us what He demands. . . .

"We are accepted by God, not because we have offered worthy
worship, but in spite of our unworthiness, because He has provided
for us a Worship, a Way, a Sacrifice, a Forerunner in Christ our
Leader and Representative, and our worship is our joyful Amen to
that Worship. This is the heart of all true Christian worship. It is our
response of faith to God's grace. So we worship God 'through Jesus

God in His grace has provided the Spirit of His Son to connect us to Christ, to actuate and motivate our participation in Christ's perfect worship.[54] The Torrance brothers have also spoken eloquently to this role of the Spirit.[55]

How precious are all the provisions of God's grace! May we sense this as deeply as Augustine did:

> My whole hope is in Thy exceeding great mercy
> and that alone. Give what Thou commandest
> and command what Thou wilt.[56]

Christ our Lord', and pray 'in the name of Jesus Christ'" (James B. Torrance, "The Place of Jesus Christ in Worship," 352).

54. Another way of stating this truth is: We *can* come to God in worship because of the work of Christ; we *want* to come to God in worship because of the work of the Holy Spirit.

55. "In the Spirit our prayer and worship participate in ways beyond our understanding in the prayer and worship of the glorified Christ" (T. F. Torrance, *Theology in Reconciliation*, 184). "The Holy Spirit enables us to enter through the veil of the flesh of Christ into the holiest, and connects us with Christ as He dwells in the immediate presence of God in unbroken communion" (Ibid., 140). "The presence of His Spirit in us means that Christ's prayer and worship of the Father are made to echo in us and issue out of our life to the Father as our own prayer and worship" (Ibid., 209). "In our human, frail, broken, unworthy response, the Spirit helps in our infirmities, lifting us up to Christ who, in his ascended *humanity*, is our God-given response, the leader of our worship, the pioneer of our faith, our advocate and high priest, who through the eternal Spirit presents us with himself to the Father. So in and through the mediatorial ministry of the Spirit, we worship the Father in the name of Christ" (James B. Torrance, *Worship, Community and the Triune God of Grace*, 88). James Torrance goes on to describe how parallel and intertwined the ministry of the Spirit is with the present ministry of Christ as a sort of "co-mediator" and "co-intercessor" (Rom 8:26) (Ibid.).

56. Augustine, *Confessions*, X.29.

10. Our singing Savior shows us the appropriateness and necessity of our own songs of praise.

As stated before, we have not fulfilled the purpose for which we were created and redeemed until we have both understood the gospel of the Lord Jesus Christ *and* responded to it with the praises due to the Father of grace.[57] And Jesus enables and empowers that response, as Poythress writes: "Christ is the leader, the model, and the motivator of New Testament congregational singing."[58]

And Paul in Romans 15:9, similarly to what we see in Hebrews 2:12, quotes from the Psalms as the very words of Jesus: "'Therefore I will praise you among the Gentiles, and sing to your name'" (Ps 18:49).

If Christ our Mediator deems it fitting to sing the Father's praises in the midst of the congregation (and among the nations), how can we do less? Ferguson and Kidd would agree:

> We come for worship to be led by one Songleader, our Lord Jesus Christ. Which, incidentally, is one of the reasons you ought to be singing. Shame on me if I am silent when I am standing at the shoulder of my Lord Jesus

---

57. This worldwide purpose of God-glorifying song is seen clearly in the Psalter: "I will give thanks to you, O Lord, among the peoples; I will sing praises to you among the nations" (57:9). "Shout for joy to God, all the earth; sing the glory of his name; give to him glorious praise! Say to God, 'How awesome are your deeds! So great is your power that your enemies come cringing to you. All the earth worships you and sings praises to you; they sing praises to your name'" (66:1–4). "Let the peoples praise you, O God; let all the peoples praise you! Let the nations be glad and sing for joy, for you judge the peoples with equity and guide the nations upon earth" (67:3). "O kingdoms of the earth, sing to God; sing praises to the Lord" (68:32). "I will give thanks to you, O LORD, among the peoples; I will sing praises to you among the nations" (108:3).

58. Poythress, "Ezra 3 (Concluded)," 218.

> Christ singing His heart out in praises to His heavenly Father. Shame on me if I am in His choir and I am silent when He is urging me to sing the praises of this magnificent God. It is a marvelous incentive to sing that you know that it is Jesus who is leading your singing.[59]

> Somehow our singing is more his than ours. It is unspeakable joy for me to take my place as a worshipper among my brothers and sisters, knowing that Jesus, the Chief Liturgist, has already taken his place.[60]

Christ our Brother and Worship Leader and bids us to join Him in singing praises to our God and Father. Calvin writes:

> As soon as God becomes known to us His infinite praises resound in our hearts and ears. And Christ encourages us by His example to sing them publicly. . . . This teaching is the very strongest encouragement to us to bring yet more fervent zeal to the praise of God, when we hear that Christ heeds our praise, and is the chief Conductor of our hymns.[61]

11. We need to consider a Christocentric view of illumination.

Hebrews 2:12's description of the continuing revelatory ministry of Christ lends credence to Ramm's view of the dynamic role of the Son in illumination.

---

59. Ferguson, "True Spirituality, True Worship."

60. Kidd, *With One Voice*, 94.

61. Calvin, *Hebrews and the First and Second Epistles of St. Peter*, 27.

Should we think that revelation is now accomplished through illumination, by the Spirit of Christ, of the written record of that once-for-all revelation? A problem with this way of stating the matter is that it has no *immediate* reference to the Lord and Prophet of the Church. How is Jesus still, in a dynamic sense, the light of the world, the prophet of the Lord, and the revealer of God? . . .

Here I make a suggestion for the broadening or deepening of the common Protestant approach to Scripture and revelation. First, we must be clear that God has spoken and that this Word has been recorded in the words of men in the books of the Bible. Yet God continues to speak the same Word to, as well as in and through, Jesus Christ, who is the same yesterday, today, and forever. Revelation happens continuously in the human mode of consciousness of our Savior in heaven. We Christians on earth who are the people of God, the body of Christ, and the household of faith, are united to our exalted Prophet and Savior as the people whom he has redeemed. In and by the Spirit, who proceeds from the Father to us through him, there is a union between the Lord in heaven and his body in heaven and on earth. . . . Rather than thinking of the Holy Spirit as shining a light on the sacred page so that individually the people of God (led by their pastors and teachers) can understand it and thereby receive the living word of God (illumination), it is preferable to say something different. The meaning of the sacred text is that meaning which God intended and which Christ has perfectly made his own. . . . Only Jesus Christ as Prophet has

fully appropriated the meaning of the revelation of God as recorded in Scripture. Therefore,
in spiritual union with his people (that is,
through the direct agency of the Holy Spirit)
that meaning which is in the human mode of
consciousness of our exalted Prophet is shared
with his people as they read the Bible or hear
it expounded. Thus the illumination is not of
the sacred page as such, but is of the mind and
heart of the pastor, teacher, or believer; and it
is by the Spirit who comes from the Lord Jesus
(see Eph 1:17,18; 3:16–17).[62]

12. We need to repent of trying to do worship in our own
strength.

Given what we have seen, it is evident that James
Torrance is right in decrying much of our evangelical understanding and practice of worship, namely:

> Worship is something which we, religious
> people, do—mainly in church on Sunday. We
> go to church, we sing our psalms and hymns to
> God, we intercede for the world, we listen to
> the sermon . . , we offer our money, time and
> talents to God. No doubt we need God's grace
> to help us do it. We do it because Jesus taught
> us to do it and left us an example of how to do
> it. But worship is what *we* do before God.
>
> In theological language, this means that the
> only priesthood is our priesthood, the only of-
> fering our offering, the only intercessions our
> intercessions.
>
> Indeed this view of worship is in practice uni-
> tarian, has no doctrine of the Mediator or Sole
> Priesthood of Christ, is human-centred, with no

62. Ramm, *An Evangelical Christology*, 94–96. His full treatment
of the subject encompasses pages 92–98.

proper doctrine of the Holy Spirit, is too often non-sacramental, and can engender weariness. We sit in the pew watching the minister "doing his thing", exhorting us "to do our thing", until we go home thinking we have done our duty for another week! This [is] do-it-yourself-with-the-help-of-the-minister worship.[63]

How this approach denigrates the marvelous provision of God's grace for our worship through the mediation of our living High Priest and the power of the Holy Spirit! How it impoverishes our worship! We need to embrace Torrance's perspective:

Worship is rather the gift of participating through the Spirit in the (incarnate) Son's communion with the Father—of participating, in union with Christ, in what he has done for us once and for all in his self-offering to the Father in his life and death on the Cross, and in what he is continuing to do for us in the presence of the Father, and in his mission from the Father to the world. There is only one offering which is truly acceptable to God, and it is not ours. It is the offering by which he has sanctified for all time those who come to God by him (Heb. 2:11; 10:10, 14). There is only one who can lead us into the presence of the Father by his sacrifice on the cross. . . .

This view is Trinitarian and incarnational. It takes seriously the New Testament teaching about the sole priesthood and headship of Christ, his self-offering for us to the Father and our life in union with Christ through the

63. James B. Torrance, *Worship, Community and the Triune God of Grace*, 20.

Spirit, with a vision of the Church as the body of Christ. . . .

Whereas the first view can be divisive, in that every church and denomination "does its own thing" and worships God in its own way, the second is unifying, in that it recognises that there is only one way to come to the Father, namely through Christ in the communion of saints, whatever outward form our worship may take. If the first way can engender weariness, this second way, the way of grace, releases joy and ecstasy. With inward peace we are lifted up by the Spirit into the presence of the Father, into a life of wonderful communion, into a life of praise and adoration in union with Christ. We know that the living Christ is in our midst, leading our worship, our prayers and our praises. . . .

The real agent in worship, in a New Testament understanding, is Jesus Christ who leads us in our praise and prayers, "the one true minister of the sanctuary," the *leitourgos ton hagion* (Heb. 8:1, 2). He is the High Priest who, by his one offering of himself for us on the cross, now leads us into the Holy of Holies, the holy presence of the Father.[64]

May our response to what we have seen be that which Thomas Torrance describes as the only appropriate one:

Through, with and in Christ we turn away in penitential self-denial from our own acts of worship and prayer in order to rest in the worship and prayer which our Saviour has already offered and continues to offer to the Father on our behalf.[65]

64. Ibid., 20–23.
65. Torrance, "The Mind of Christ in Worship," 211–12.

Conclusion

I T HAS been said that "Christianity is Christ." An important corollary of that statement may be drawn from the above study: "New Testament worship is Christ." As Nicholls states it:

> Christ is the essence of worship, and our understanding of the Church's worship must take its starting point from Him. In Him is embodied the downward movement of God's love and grace, as He reveals Himself to man, and reconciles man to Himself; and also the upward movement of man's response, perfectly dependent upon that love, and drawing from it all the resources of strength which are needed to make that response in all circumstances of life, and even in death itself.[1]

All true worship is in and through and by Jesus Christ. This is a supremely unifying understanding of Christian worship in all times and places and styles and forms. Our oneness in worship is predicated upon the Father's answer to the amazing prayer which Jesus made on our behalf on the night before He was crucified: "even as You, Father, are in Me and I in You, that they also may be in Us." Our great High Priest and older Brother draws us into the fellowship of the Trinity itself . . . where all is one in everlasting love and selfless communion.

May His will be done on earth as it is in heaven!

1. Nicholls, *Jacob's Ladder*, 26.

Bibliography

Abba, Raymond. *Principles of Christian Worship*. New York: Oxford University Press, 1957.

Alexander, Eric. *Worship: The Old Testament Pattern*. Philadelphia Conference on Reformed Theology, 2002. Audiocassette.

Archer, Gleason L., Jr. *The Epistle to the Hebrews: A Study Manual*. Grand Rapids: Baker Book House, 1957.

Augustine. *The Confessions of St. Augustine*. New York: The New American Library, 1963.

Bales, James D. *Studies in Hebrews*. Shreveport, Louisiana: Lambert Book House, 1972.

Barclay, William. *The Letter to the Hebrews*. 2nd edition. The Daily Study Bible. Philadelphia: The Westminster Press, 1957.

Barnes, Albert. "Hebrews." In *Notes on the New Testament Explanatory and Practical*. Grand Rapids: Baker Book House, 1966.

Barrett, C. K. *A Commentary on the Epistle to the Romans*. Harper New Testament Commentaries. New York: Harper & Bros., 1957.

Bateman, Herbert W., IV. *Early Jewish Hermeneutics and Hebrews 1:5–13: The Impact of Early Jewish Exegesis on the Interpretation of a Significant New Testament Passage*. American University Studies: Series VII: Theology and Religion. New York: Peter Lang, 1997.

Bauer, Walter. *A Greek–English Lexicon of the New Testament and Other Early Christian Literature*. Translated and adapted by William F. Arndt and F. Wilbur Gingrich, 1957. Second edition, revised and augmented by F. Wilbur Gingrich and Frederick W. Danker. Chicago: University of Chicago Press, 1979.

Bengel, John Albert. *Gnomon of the New Testament*. Volume 4. Translated by Andrew R. Fausset. Edinburgh: T. & T. Clark, 1866.

Blass, F. and A. Debrunner. *A Greek Grammar of the New Testament and Other Early Christian Literature*. Translated and edited by Robert W. Funk. Chicago: University of Chicago Press, 1961.

Blaszczak, Gerald R. *A Formcritical Study of Selected Odes of Solomon.* Harvard Semitic Monographs, edited by Frank Moore. Atlanta: Scholars Press, 1985.

Brown, John. *An Exposition of the Epistle to the Hebrews.* Second edition. London: The Banner of Truth Trust, 1964.

Bruce, Alexander Balmain. *The Epistle to the Hebrews: The First Apology for Christianity (an Exegetical Study).* Edinburgh: T. & T. Clark, 1899.

Bruce, F. F. *The Epistle to the Hebrews.* The New International Commentary on the New Testament, edited by F. F. Bruce. Grand Rapids: Wm. B. Eerdmans Publishing Co., 1964.

———. *What the Bible Teaches About What Jesus Did.* What the Bible Teaches About, edited by G. W. Kirby. Wheaton: Tyndale House Publishers, 1979.

Butin, Philip W. *Reformed Ecclesiology: Trinitarian Grace According to Calvin.* Studies in Reformed Theology and History, edited by David Willis-Watkins. Princeton: Princeton Theological Seminary, 1994.

———. *Revelation, Redemption, and Response: Calvin's Trinitarian Understanding of the Divine-Human Relationship.* New York: Oxford University Press, 1995.

Calvin, John. *Commentaries on the Epistle to the Hebrews.* Translated by John Owen. Grand Rapids: Wm. B. Eerdmans Publishing Co., 1949.

———. *The Epistle of Paul the Apostle to the Hebrews and the First and Second Epistles of St. Peter.* Translated by William B. Johnston. Calvin's Commentaries, edited by Thomas F. Torrance and David W. Torrance. Grand Rapids: Wm. B. Eerdmans Publishing Co., 1963.

Calvin, John *Institutes of the Christian Religion.* Richmond, Virginia: John Knox Press, 1975.

Chafer, Lewis Sperry. *Major Bible Themes.* Revised by John F. Walvoord. Grand Rapids: Zondervan Publishing House, 1974.

Chirichigno, Gleason L Archer and Gregory. *Old Testament Quotations in the New Testament.* Chicago: Moody Press, 1983.

Clowney, Edmund P. "The Singing Savior." *Moody Monthly* July/August 1979, 40–42.

Cocksworth, Christopher. *Holy, Holy, Holy: Worshipping the Trinitarian God.* Trinity and Truth Series, edited by Stephen Sykes. London: Darton, Longman and Todd, 1997.

Craigie, Peter C. *Psalms 1–50*. Volume 19, Word Biblical Commentary, edited by David A. Hubbard and Glenn W. Barker. Waco, Texas: Word Books, 1983.

Cranfield, C. E. B. *A Critical and Exegetical Commentary on the Epistle to the Romans*. 2 volumes. International Critical Commentary, Edinburgh: T. & T. Clark, 1979.

Dale, R. W. *The Jewish Temple and the Christian Church: A Series of Discourses on the Epistle to the Hebrews*. Eleventh edition. London: Hodder & Stoughton, 1902.

Davidson, Robert. *The Vitality of Worship: A Commentary on the Book of Psalms*. Grand Rapids: William B. Eerdmans Publishing Company, 1998.

Davies, J. H. *A Letter to Hebrews*. The Cambridge Bible Commentary, edited by P. R. Ackroyd, A. R. C. Leaney, and J. W. Packer. Cambridge, England: At the University Press, 1967.

Delitzsch, F. and C.F. Keil. *Psalms*, In Commentary of the Old Testament, edited by F. Delitzsch. Reprint, Grand Rapids: William B. Eerdmans Publishing Company, 1976.

Delitzsch, Franz. *Commentary on the Epistle to the Hebrews*. Translated by Thomas L. Kingsbury. Vol. 1, Clark's Foreign Theological Library. Edinburgh: T. & T. Clark, 1878.

DeSilva, David A. *Perseverance in Gratitude: A Socio-Rhetorical Commentary on the Epistle "To the Hebrews."* Grand Rapids: Wm. B. Eerdmans Publishing Co., 2000.

Doormann, Friedrich. "Deinen Namen will ich meinen Brüdern verkünden (Hebr. 2,11-13)." *Bibel im Leben* 14 (1973): 245–52.

Ebrard, John H. A. *Biblical Commentary on the Epistle to the Hebrews*. Clark's Foreign Theological Library. Edinburgh: T. & T. Clark, 1853.

Eisenbaum, Pamela Michelle. *The Jewish Heroes of Christian History: Hebrews 11 in Literary Context*. Society of Biblical Literature Dissertation Series, edited by Michael V. Fox (OT Editor) and Pheme Perkins (NT Editor). Atlanta: Scholars Press, 1997.

Ellingworth, Paul. *The Epistle to the Hebrews*. Epworth Commentaries, edited by Harold F. Guite and Ivor H. Jones. London: Epworth Press, 1991.

———. *The Epistle to the Hebrews*. The New International Greek Testament Commentary, edited by I. Howard Marshall and W. Ward Gasque. Grand Rapids: Wm. B. Eerdmans Publishing Co., 1993.

The Epistle of Barnabas. Translated by Kirsopp Lake. Vol. 1 of The Apostolic Fathers. Cambridge, Massachusetts: Harvard University Press, 1952.

Farrar, F. W. *The Epistle of Paul the Apostle to the Hebrews.* Cambridge Greek Testament for Schools and Colleges, edited by J. J. S. Perowne. Cambridge, England: At the University Press, 1888.

Farris, Stephen. "Reformed Identity and Reformed Worship." *Reformed World* 43, no. 1&2 (1993): 69–76.

Ferguson, Sinclair. "The Church's Worship." Orlando: Ligonier Conference, 2006. Audio Message.

———. "True Spirituality, True Worship." Lookout Mountain GA: Covenant College, 2004. Audio CD.

Furr, Gary and Milburn Price. *The Dialogue of Worship: Creating Space for Revelation and Response.* Macon, Georgia: Smyth & Helwys, 1998.

Gese, Hartmut. "Psalm 22 und das Neue Testament." *Zeitschrift für Theologie und Kirche* 65 (1968): 1-22.

Glodo, Michael. "Singing with the Savior." *RTS Reformed Journal* 17, no. 1 (1998). Available at www.rts.edu/quarterly/spring98/glodo.html.

Gooding, David. *An Unshakeable Kingdom: The Letter to the Hebrews for Today.* Grand Rapids: Wm. B. Eerdmans Publishing Co., 1989.

Goodspeed, Edgar J. *The Epistle to the Hebrews.* The Bible for Home and School. New York: The MacMillan Company, 1908.

Gordon, Robert P. *Hebrews.* Readings: A New Biblical Commentary, edited by John Jarick. Sheffield, England: Sheffield Academic Press, 2000.

Grant, Frederick C. *The Epistle to the Hebrews.* Harper's Annotated Bible, edited by Julius A. Bewer and Frederick C. Grant. New York: Harper and Brothers, 1956.

Greenlee, J. Harold. *An Exegetical Summary of Hebrews.* Dallas: Summer Institute of Linguistics, 1998.

Grudem, Wayne. *Systematic Theology.* Grand Rapids: Zondervan Publishing House, 1994.

Hageman, Howard. "Can Church Music Be Reformed?" *The Reformed Review* 14, no. 2 (1960):19-28.

Harlow, R. E. *Basic Bible Doctrines.* Emmaus Correspondence Courses. Oak Park, Illinois: Emmaus Bible School, 1968, 1972.

Hewitt, Thomas. *The Epistle to the Hebrews.* The Tyndale New Testament Commentaries, edited by R. V. G. Tasker. Grand Rapids: Wm. B. Eerdmans Publishing Co., 1960.

Hilber, John W. "Theology of Worship in Exodus 24." *Journal of the Evangelical Theological Society* 39, no. 2 (1996): 177–89.

The Holy Bible, English Standard Version. Wheaton IL: Crossway Bibles, 2001. Used by permission. All rights reserved.

Hughes, Graham. *Hebrews and Hermeneutics: The Epistle to the Hebrews as a New Testament Example of Biblical Interpretation.* Society for New Testament Studies Monograph Series, edited by R. McL. Wilson. Cambridge, England: Cambridge University Press, 1979.

Hughes, Philip Edgcomb. *A Commentary on the Epistle to the Hebrews.* Grand Rapids: Wm. B. Eerdmans Publishing Co., 1977.

Isaacs, Marie E. *Sacred Space: An Approach to the Theology of the Epistle to the Hebrews.* Journal for the Study of the New Testament Supplement Series. Sheffield, England: JSOT Press, 1992.

Johnsson, William G. *Hebrews.* Knox Preaching Guides, edited by John H. Hayes. Atlanta: John Knox Press, 1980.

Jordan, Clarence. *The Cotton Patch Version of Hebrews and the General Epistles.* New York: Association Press, 1973.

Jungmann, Josef A. *The Place of Christ in Liturgical Prayer.* Translated by Geoffrey Chapman. Classics in Liturgy. Collegeville, Minnesota: The Liturgical Press, 1965.

Kendrick, A. C. *Commentary on the Epistle to the Hebrews.* Philadelphia: American Baptist Publication Society, 1889.

Kidd, Reggie M. "Bach, Bubba, and the Blues Brothers." *RTS Reformed Journal* 18, no. 2 (1998).

———. *With One Voice: Discovering Christ's Song in Our Worship.* Grand Rapids: Baker Books, 2005.

Kidner, Derek. *Psalms 1–72.* Tyndale Old Testament Commentaries, edited by D.J. Wiseman. London: Inter-Varsity Press, 1973.

Kistemaker, Simon. *Exposition of the Epistle to the Hebrews.* New Testament Commentary. Grand Rapids: Baker Book House, 1984.

———. *The Psalm Citation in the Epistle to the Hebrews.* Amsterdam: Wed. G. Van Soest N.V., 1961.

Koester, Craig R. *Hebrews.* Vol. 36, The Anchor Bible. New York: Doubleday, 2001.

Kovach, Stephen D., and Peter R. Schemm, Jr. "A Defense of the Doctrine of the Eternal Subordination of the Son." *Journal of the Evangelical Theological Society* 42 (1999):461-76.

Lane, William L. *Call to Commitment: Responding to the Message of Hebrews.* Nashville: Thomas Nelson, 1985.

————. *Hebrews 1–8*. Word Biblical Commentary, edited by David A. Hubbard, Glenn W. Barker, and Ralph P. Martin. Dallas: Word Books, 1991.

Lang, G. H. *The Epistle to the Hebrews: A Practical Treatise for Plain and Serious Readers*. London: The Paternoster Press, 1951.

Lange, Harvey D. "The Relationship between Psalm 22 and the Passion Narrative." *Concordia Theological Monthly* 43 (1972): 610–21.

Lenski, R. C. H. *The Interpretation of the Epistle to the Hebrews and the Epistle of James*. Columbus, Ohio: The Wartburg Press, 1946.

Leonard, William. *Authorship of the Epistle to the Hebrews: Critical Problem and Use of the Old Testament*. Rome: Vatican Polyglot Press, 1939.

Lewis, C. S. "On Church Music." In *Christian Reflections*. Grand Rapids: Wm. B. Eerdmans Publishing Co., 1967.

Liesch, Barry. *The New Worship: Straight Talk on Music and the Church (Expanded Edition)*. Grand Rapids: Baker Books, 1995, 2001.

Lightfoot, J. B. *Saint Paul's Epistles to the Colossians and to Philemon*. Zondervan Commentary Series. Grand Rapids: Zondervan Publishing House, 1879. Reprint, 14th printing, 1978.

Lightfoot, Neil R. *Jesus Christ Today: A Commentary on the Book of Hebrews*. Grand Rapids: Baker Book House, 1976.

Mains, Karen Burton. "Introduction." In *Sing Joyfully* (Hymnal), edited by Jack Schrader. Carol Stream, Illinois: Tabernacle Publishing Company, 1989.

Man, Ronald E. "Yes and Amen." http://www.worr.org/?page_id=23.

Martyr, Justin. *First Apology*. Translated by Leslie William Barnard. Ancient Christian Writers, edited by Walter J. Burghardt, John J. Dillon, and Dennis D. McManus. New York: Paulist Press, 1997.

Mays, James Luther. *Psalms*. Interpretation: A Bible Commentary for Teaching and Preaching, edited by James L. Mays. Louisville: John Knox Press, 1994.

Michel, Otto. *Der Brief an die Hebräer*. Kritisch-Exegetischer Kommentar über das Neue Testament. Göttingen: Vandenhoeck & Ruprecht, 1966.

Miller, Patrick D. *Interpreting the Psalms*. Philadelphia: Fortress Press, 1986.

Milligan, R. *Epistle to the Hebrews*. The New Testament Commentary. Cincinnati: The Standard Publishing Company, n.d.

Moffatt, James. *A Critical and Exegetical Commentary on the Epistle to the Hebrews.* The International Critical Commentary. Edinburgh: T. & T. Clark, 1924.

Montefiore, Hugh. *A Commentary on the Epistle to the Hebrews.* Harper's New Testament Commentaries, edited by Henry Chadwick. New York: Harper & Row, 1964.

Morris, Leon. *The Epistle to the Romans.* Pillar New Testament Commentary. Grand Rapids: Wm. B. Eerdmans Publishing Co., 1988.

Müller, D. "Apostle." In *New International Dictionary of New Testament Theology,* edited by Colin Brown. Grand Rapids: Zondervan, 1986.

Murray, Andrew. *The Holiest of All: An Exposition of the Epistle to the Hebrews.* Old Tappan, New Jersey: Fleming H. Revell, 1960.

Murray, John. *The Epistle to the Romans.* New International Commentary on the New Testament. Grand Rapids: Wm. B. Eerdmans Publishing Co., 1959.

———. "The Heavenly, Priestly Activity of Christ." In *The Claims of Truth,* 44–58. Edinburgh: Banner of Truth Trust, 1976.

———. "The Living Saviour." In *The Claims of Truth,* 40–43. Edinburgh: Banner of Truth Trust, 1976.

Nairn, Alexander. *The Epistle of Priesthood: Studies in the Epistle to the Hebrews.* Edinburgh: T. & T. Clark, 1913.

Nairne, A. *The Epistle to the Hebrews.* Cambridge Greek Testament for Schools and Colleges, edited by R. St. John Parry. Cambridge, England: At the University Press, 1922.

Newell, William R. *Hebrews Verse by Verse.* 2nd edition. Chicago, Illinois: Moody Press, 1947.

Nicholls, William. *Jacob's Ladder: The Meaning of Worship.* Ecumenical Studies in Worship. Richmond, Virginia: John Knox Press, 1958.

O'Brien, Peter T. *Colossians, Philemon.* Vol. 44, Word Biblical Commentary, edited by Ralph P. Martin. Waco, Texas: Word Books, 1982.

Owen, John. *An Exposition of the Epistle to the Hebrews.* Volume 3 of 7 (Hebrews 1:1—3:6). Grand Rapids: Baker Book House, 1980.

Packer, J. I. Packer and Coates, R. J. *Beyond the Battle for the Bible.* Westchester, Illinois: Cornerstone Books, 1980.

Patterson, Ben. *Serving God: The Grand Essentials of Work and Worship.* 1987. Revised edition. Downers Grove, Illinois: InterVarsity Press, 1994.

Perowne, J. J. Stewart. *The Book of Psalms*. Volume 1 of 2. Andover, Massachusetts: Warren F. Draper, 1882.

Peterson, David. *Hebrews and Perfection: An Examination of the Concept of Perfection in the 'Epistle to the Hebrews'*. Cambridge, England: Cambridge University Press, 1982.

Pfitzner, Victor C. *Hebrews*. Abingdon New Testament Commentaries, edited by Victor Paul Furnish. Nashville: Abingdon Press, 1997.

Pink, Arthur W. *An Exposition of Hebrews*. 1954. Reprint, Grand Rapids: Baker Book House, 1968.

Poythress, Vern S. "Ezra 3, Union with Christ, and Exclusive Psalmody." *Westminster Theological Journal* 37, no. 1 (1975): 74-94.

————. "Ezra 3, Union with Christ, and Exclusive Psalmody (Concluded)." *Westminster Theological Journal* 37, no. 2 (1975): 218-35.

Ramm, Bernard L. *An Evangelical Christology: Ecumenic and Historic*. Nashville: Thomas Nelson Publishers, 1985.

Rawlinson, A. E. J. *The New Testament Doctrine of the Christ*. London: Longmans, Green and Co., 1926.

Rengstorf, Karl Heinrich. "ἀπόστολος." In *Theological Dictionary of the New Testament*, edited by Gerhard Kittel. Grand Rapids: Wm. B. Eerdmans Publishing Co., 1964.

Riggenbach, D. Eduard. *Der Brief an Die Hebräer*. Kommentar zum Neuen Testament, edited by Theodor Zahn. Leipzig: A. Deichert'sche Verlagsbuchhandlung, 1913.

Saphir, Adolph. *The Epistle to the Hebrews: An Exposition*. Volume 1 of 2. 2nd American edition, New York: Fleming H. Revell, 1902.

————. *The Great High Priest: An Exposition of the Epistle to the Hebrews*. Glasgow: Pickering & Inglis, n.d.

Schierse, F. J. *The Epistle to the Hebrews*. New Testament for Spiritual Reading, edited by John L. McKenzie. London: Burns & Oates, 1964.

Schneider, Johannes. *The Letter to the Hebrews*. Translated by William A. Mueller. Grand Rapids: Wm. B. Eerdmans Publishing Co., 1957.

Scott, E. F. *The Epistle to the Hebrews: Its Doctrine and Significance*. Edinburgh: T. & T. Clark, 1922.

Sexton, Marcus L. *Exposition of Hebrews, Jude, and Philemon*. Pottersville, Missouri: Scaggs Publications, 1996.

Simpson, E. K. "The Vocabulary of the Epistle to the Hebrews." *Evangelical Quarterly* 18, no. 3 (1946):187-90.

Simpson, E. K. and F. F. Bruce. *Commentary on the Epistles to the Ephesians and the Colossians*. New International Commentary of the New Testament, edited by F. F. Bruce. Grand Rapids: Wm. B. Eerdmans Publishing Co., 1957.

Smith, Robert H. *Hebrews*. Augsburg Commentary on the New Testament. Minneapolis: Augsburg Publishing House, 1984.

Sowers, Sidney G. *The Hermeneutics of Philo and Hebrews*. Basel Studies of Theology. Zurich: EVZ-Verlag, 1965.

Spurgeon, Charles Haddon. *The Treasury of David*. http://www.spurgeon.org/treasury/ps022.htm.

Stedman, Ray C. *Hebrews*. The IVP New Testament Commentary Series, edited by Grant R. Osborne. Downers Grove, Illinois: InterVarsity Press, 1992.

Stibbs, Alan M. *So Great Salvation: The Meaning and Message of the Letter to the Hebrews*, The Christian Student's Library. Exeter, England: The Paternoster Press, 1970.

Stott, John. *Romans: God's Good News for the World*. The Bible Speaks Today. Downers Grove, Illinois: InterVarsity Press, 1994.

Swetnam, James. *Jesus and Isaac: A Study of the Epistle to the Hebrews in the Light of the Aqedah*. Analecta Biblica. Rome: Biblical Institute Press, 1981.

Synge, F. C. *Hebrews and the Scriptures*. London: S.P.C.K., 1959.

Tait, William. *Meditationes Hebraicae, or, a Doctrinal and Practical Exposition of the Epistle of St. Paul to the Hebrews*. London: Seeley, Burnside and Seeley, 1845.

Tasker, R. V. G. *The Gospel in the Epistle to the Hebrews*. London: The Tyndale Press, 1950.

Toon, Peter. *Our Triune God: A Biblical Portrayal of the Trinity*. Wheaton: Victor Books/SP Publications, 1996.

Torrance, James B. "Christ in Our Place: The Joy of Worship." In *A Passion for Christ: The Vision That Ignites Ministry*, edited by Gerrit Dawson and Jock Stein. Lenoir, North Carolina: PLC Publications, 1999.

———. "The Doctrine of the Trinity in Our Contemporary Situation." In *The Forgotten Trinity*, edited by Alasdair I.C. Heron. London: BCC/CCBI, 1991.

———. "The Place of Jesus Christ in Worship." In *Theological Foundations for Ministry*, edited by Ray S. Anderson. Grand Rapids: Wm. B. Eerdmans Publishing Co., 1979.

———. *Worship, Community and the Triune God of Grace*. Downers Grove, Illinois: InterVarsity Press, 1996.

————. "The Contribution of John McLeod Campbell to Scottish Theology." *Scottish Journal of Theology* 26, no. 3 (1973): 295–311.

Torrance, Thomas F. *The Mediation of Christ*. Grand Rapids: Wm. B. Eerdmans Publishing Co., 1983.

————. "The Mind of Christ in Worship: The Problem of Apollinarianism in the Liturgy." In *Theology in Reconciliation*. Grand Rapids: Wm. B. Eerdmans Publishing Co., 1975.

————. *Royal Priesthood*. Edinburgh: Tweeddale Court, 1955.

————. *Theology in Reconstruction*. London: SCM Press, 1965.

Tozer, A. W. *Worship: The Missing Jewel*. Classic Christian Living Series. Reprint, Camp Hill, Pennsylvania: Christian Publications, 1992.

VanGemeren, Willem A. *Psalms*. Volume 5 of The Expositor's Bible Commentary, edited by Frank E. Gaebelein. Grand Rapids: Zondervan, 1991.

Vaughan, C. J. *The Epistle to the Hebrews*. New York: MacMillan and Co., 1891.

Vos, Geerhardus. *The Teaching of the Epistle to the Hebrews*. Edited and rewritten by Johannes G. Vos. Grand Rapids: Wm. B. Eerdmans Publ. Co., 1956.

Wainwright, Geoffrey. *Doxology: The Praise of God in Worship, Doctrine, and Life: A Systematic Theology*. New York: Oxford University Press, 1980.

————. "The Praise of God in the Theological Reflection of the Church." *Interpretation* 39 (1985):34–45 .

Webber, Robert A. "A Blended Worship Response." In *Exploring the Worship Spectrum*, edited by Paul A. Basden. Grand Rapids: Zondervan Publishing House, 2004.

————."Blended Worship." In *Exploring the Worship Spectrum*, edited by Paul A. Basden. Grand Rapids: Zondervan Publishing House, 2004.

————. *Worship Old and New*. Grand Rapids: Zondervan Publishing House, 1982.

Weiss, Bernhard. *Kritisch Exegetisches Handbuch über den Brief an Die Hebräer*. Kritisch Exegetischer Kommentar über das Neue Testament, edited by Heinrich Augustus Wilhelm Meyer. Göttingen: Vandenhoeck und Ruprecht, 1888.

Westcott, Brooke Foss. *The Epistle to the Hebrews*. Grand Rapids: Wm. B. Eerdmans Publishing Co., 1955.

Westermann, Claus. *Praise and Lament in the Psalms.* Translated by Keith R. Crim and Richard N. Soulen. Atlanta: John Knox Press, 1981.

———. *The Psalms: Structure, Content and Message.* Minneapolis: Augsburg Publishing House, 1980.

White, James F. "Making Our Worship More Biblical." *Perkins Journal* 34 (1980): 38-40.

———. "The Missing Jewel of the Evangelical Church." In *Christian Worship in North America, a Retrospective: 1955–95.* Collegeville, Minnesota: The Liturgical Press, 1997.

Wickham, E. C. *The Epistle to the Hebrews.* London: Methuen & Co., 1910.

Williams, R. R. *Reading through Hebrews.* London: A. R. Mowbray & Co., 1961.

Williamson, Ronald. *The Epistle to the Hebrews.* Epworth Preacher's Commentaries. London: The Epworth Press, 1964.

Willson, Sanders L. "Receiving Jesus as Priest." Memphis, TN: Second Presbyterian Church. Sermon.

Wilson, R. McLean. *Hebrews.* New Century Bible Commentary, edited by Ronald E. Clements and Matthew Black. Grand Rapids: Wm. B. Eerdmans Publishing Co., 1987.

Windisch, Hans. *Der Hebräerbrief.* Handbuch zum Neuen Testament, edited by Hans Lietzmann. Tübingen: J. C. B. Mohr, 1931.

Wuest, Kenneth S. *Hebrews in the Greek New Testament for the English Reader.* Grand Rapids: Wm. B. Eerdmans Publ. Co., 1956.

Scripture Index